MALE / FEMALE LANGUAGE

With a comprehensive bibliography

by
Mary Ritchie Key

The Scarecrow Press, Inc.
Metuchen, N.J.   1975

Library of Congress Cataloging in Publication Data

Key, Mary Ritchie.
   Male/female language, with a comprehensive
bibliography.

   Bibliography: p.
   1. Sociolinguistics. 2. Sex (Psychology) I.
I. Title.
P40.K4   301.2'1   74-19105
ISBN 0-8108-0748-3

TABLE OF CONTENTS

PREFACE

Not another book on women!

The difference today is that now the books about
women are being written by women. This should enhance
the information and perspectives on the problems of human
relationships. Here we might recall the old fable about
the lion and the painting. The story goes that a lion was
looking at a painting of a hunter slaying a lion, and he commented, "Yes, but who painted the picture? A lion might
have done it differently." As I researched the linguistic
studies on "women's language," it became abundantly clear
that men were left out. Note the many titles in the bibliography which refer only to women's language. Often the
studies simply reiterated the old saw that women were
peculiar and their speech types "abnormal" or "cute" or
somehow less than normal. Equally balanced studies of
female and male differences and varieties are needed, in
order to understand the whole.

This book is an expansion of a paper which I de-
livered at the American Dialect Society in New York in
1970. I first became aware of male/female differences in
language when I heard them many years ago in a South
American Indian language located in the rainforest of the
great Amazon region. I became seriously involved in observing male/female differences several years ago when I
initiated a course on male/female language at the University
of California. It may have been the first course on this
subject ever taught. From that course I prepared an outline and bibliography which were included in Female Studies:
No. 2, published by the Modern Language Association. I
am writing at a time when male and female usage is very
much in a state of transition. What is said today must be
revised tomorrow. Some of the examples will seem out of
date; others will be ahead of their time.

Three persons have influenced my thinking in im-
measurable ways.   Margaret Mead's work has changed the
attitude and thinking regarding male and female behavior in
all aspects of life, and the impact of her analyses continues
throughout academia.   Two others' works I first read many
years ago when I was in the process of developing the course
on male/female linguistic behavior are Simone de Beauvoir's
The Second Sex and Virginia Woolf's A Room of One's Own.
I believe the ideas from these three persons are landmarks
in a world of changing human relations and I perpetuated
their ideas with grateful abandon.   I felt especially the influence of Virginia Woolf as I wrote the last chapter.

While the courses I have taught were academically
oriented in linguistics, I have tried to write this book, in
addition, for the general reader.   Chapters VIII and IX are
most central to my field and may seem very technical, but
the general reader can walk around them and continue with
material which is of interest to all human beings in whatever vocation.   I have rigorously included documentation
and a bibliography which should be helpful to the researcher.
After many years of collecting material, I believe that the
bibliography is the most complete list on male/female
linguistic behavior in print.   In the last chapter I suggest
some areas of research which would be useful to investigate in the future for a better understanding of these sociolinguistic events.

Also in the last chapter I point toward a future that
could be rewarding to both male and female of whatever life
style.   The inextricable relationship of living and language
is a commonplace, and the dignity and well-being of all
human beings obliges the development of an androgynous
language.   A good example of the androgynous ideas that I
speak of in the last chapter is the journalist's write-up of
the Bobby Riggs and Margaret Court tennis match this year,
when it was said that the match "was a triumph for Riggs'
softly feminine style over Court's manly athletic game..."
(Newsweek, May 28, 1973, p. 77).

My list of credits, besides the bibliography, sounds
more like my course list of students, and my address book.
I have learned so much from a great many people who
were generous in responding, in bringing me examples, and
giving their own observations.   To my former students, I
want to express my indebtedness for their interest and
enthusiastic projects and papers.

Writing this book has opened up new adventures for me. One of the ones I least expected, but found most enlightening, worthwhile, stimulating, and enjoyable, was the correspondence with cartoonists as I arranged for publication. They really do have good humor! And they are most generous. One, in the course of arriving at a fair fee for reproducing his work, noted "How sad that the only currency for communication is currency." Another cartoonist sent along a quote from Baudelaire: "Each of us is a man, a woman and a child." I am very pleased to acknowledge my appreciation for them and to them.

A library is a scholar's lifeline, and I want to mention especially my own university library. Though it is small, it is unexcelled in service. My warm and joyous thanks go to Janet Eggleston and her staff for scouring the country for interlibrary loans, and to Margaret Kahn and her staff for references. The Coleridge reference was a real treasure hunt, but Ms. Kahn found it.

This little book, then, is a result of several years of teaching sociolinguistics; many years of serious linguistic research; a lifetime of knowing what it is like to be female; and a lifetime of wondering what it is like to be male.

Mary Ritchie Key
University of California, Irvine
August 1973

The truth is, a great mind must be androgynous.
                              --Coleridge

Chapter I

IN THE BEGINNING:
MALE AND FEMALE DIFFERENTIATION

There is a good principle, which has created
    order, light, and man;
and a bad principle, which has created chaos,
    darkness, and woman.
                    --attrib. to Pythagoras[1]

The separation of the roles of male and female undoubtedly goes back to the beginnings of the history of human beings for very obvious reasons: child-bearing functions. It is a safe assumption that differences in the language of male and female also go back to the beginning of
language, though we have to realize that much of history is
lost in this aspect of human affairs, as well as in all other
facets of human conduct.

Language is in a constant state of flux; today the
focus is upon changes in the area of male and female linguistic behavior. People are taking a second look at language forms which they have been using automatically all
their lives. What was always there is now being examined
carefully with pink and blue glasses. A great deal of experimentation is taking place during these transitional stages
and while some of what is being tried today will remain in
common usage, other forms will be dropped along the way.
What is happening today is a general liberation of the language. All of this is rather fascinating and frightening;
nevertheless, it is spiced with humor. The purported
"phallacies about the movement" are being avidly discussed
and there was a long and tense argument about "pronoun
envy"[2] at one of our prestigious institutions. A radio
newscaster reported that a suit was being filed on the basis
of sex discrimination because a woman was turned down for
a job as Santa Claus. He quipped that, "In order to go
HO, HO, HO, it is not necessary to be a HE, HE, HE!"

11

"Now that we've learned to talk, try to speak the same language."

By Herbert Goldberg; copyright © 1970 by Saturday Review, Inc.

A recent stage production was named, "Adam and Even." A prominent feminist published "Quotations from Charwoman Me."[3] Humor is a non-threatening way that human beings have to deal with the world about them.   It functions as a

safety valve for situations too difficult to trust oneself with.
Magnificent puns and plays on words have emanated from
this focus upon male/female problems which all students of
language will appreciate. In any case, it is quite apparent
that in these times, a woman is not apt to take a "broad"
view of things, and many hope that fewer men do.

The first time that I became aware of male/female
differences in languages, I was in Bolivia as a linguistic
consultant visiting different villages studying the various
Indian languages spoken. I landed at a little village, which
probably isn't on your map, where the Ignaciano Indians
have been living for centuries. Up until that time not much
was known about their language, and I was to verify some
of the linguistic data which had been collected. The linguist
who had written down this material was a male, and I was
reading from his field notes. I sat down on a tree stump
surrounded by large pottery vessels and chickens and children, and I read off the phonetically transcribed vocabulary
items. My informant was an affable woman who was bilingual and could tell me in Spanish what the words meant.
When I came to a certain form, she started laughing, and
I thought she was going to fall off her stool from amuse-
ment! We soon discovered that the word which I had read
was from the vocabulary of men--a word which females
never articulated.

It was several years later when I began teaching a
course on varieties of language that I began to focus again
on the differences between male and female linguistic behavior. It soon became apparent to me that this distinction
in language is a certain universal just as the sex role is
universal, and that linguistic sex distinctions undoubtedly
occur in every language of the world. Interestingly enough,
however, they have not been reported upon widely. Of the
some four to five thousand languages of the world, I can
find linguistic statements about sex distinctions in fewer than
a hundred.

Societies cannot exist without language. Yet in spite
of this universality, and even though Plato and Aristotle and
other great minds throughout the centuries have commented
on language, the science of language, or linguistics, is a
fairly recent discipline. Only in the last century or two
has linguistics (previously philology) been accepted as a
discipline in its own right on university campuses. But
the differentiated use of language by male and female is

more than just a matter of linguistic forms; it is the use
of these forms in society.   It is the sociological choice
and function of these forms.   In the early development of
linguistics, scholars were so busy trying to find symbols
for the sounds they found in languages and to define subjects and predicates that they did not have time to become
involved in the interdisciplinary efforts necessary to
systematically describe the sociologically important male
and female differences.   In addition, the differences that
occur are often very subtle and abstract, and though everyone responds to them, they are not readily identified.   If
you ask your friend, "How do men and women talk differently?" the answer is likely to be something vague:
"Well, I don't know ... do they? ... why, I suppose they
do!"

Although extensive systematic studies on male/female
linguistic distinctions were not made until this century, some
language studies from very early times did, however, make
brief mention of sex differences. [4] Mulcaster in 1582 commented on the different pronunciation by male and female
and related these differences to refined and vulgar language.
It is probably not an unrelated fact in Mulcaster's life that
he also advocated education for girls. [5] Writers on the
French language in 1688 and around 1700 made similar observations about female pronunciation.   The volubility attributed to women speakers was noted by Swift in 1735, and
a generation later Lord Chesterfield commented on women's
fondness for hyperbole: a very small gold snuff-box was
"vastly pretty, because it was so vastly little."   Oscar
Wilde continued the observations on women's speech: "Women are a decorative sex.   They never have anything to say,
but they say it charmingly."

Sometimes it is easier to observe differences ob-
jectively when the subject matter is not our own.   This
seems to be the case in linguistic studies of male/female
language, because the first statement I find with substantial
data about these differences is on the American Indian languages, Carib and Arawakan (see Chapter XIV for description), recorded by Raymond Breton in Dictionaire Caraibe-
François [sic] in 1665.   Throughout the nineteenth century descriptions are largely on "the women's language" of these exotic,
aboriginal peoples.   Travelers, historians, and philologists
such as Humboldt[6] enjoyed commenting on these esoteric
tribes where the men and women had different languages!   It
has never been true that males and females had completely

different languages, for the societies could not have existed
as such.

In this century, language scholars, notably the famous
Danish scholar, Otto Jespersen, and the great linguist, Edward Sapir, began more extensive studies of male and female
language differences. These scholars, however, were bound
by their cultural preconceptions and distortions, as all human
beings are, and this is reflected in their otherwise scholarly
treatments of "women's language." Jesperson spoke of feminine weaknesses and Sapir included women's speech in his
study of "abnormal types of speech." Greenough and Kittredge,
highly respected English scholars, spoke of "feminine peculiarities." In discussions of the German language, it was said
that, "Women naturally have certain peculiarities in their German as in other languages.... "[7]

It was shortly before this time that some scholars
had come to the conclusion that genius could only be a masculine trait. This was "documented" by Weininger, along
with his other ideas that women did not have souls and that
they were incapable of true love. [8] Not all great thinkers
were hospitable to the idea that women did not have souls;
for example, George Bernard Shaw: "Men are waking up
to the perception that in killing women's souls they have
killed their own."[9] To be fair one should say that Jespersen
tried to have a more balanced perspective about genius--and
he pointed out that "idiocy is more common among men,"[10]
another myth that he would have been unable to prove.
Nevertheless, these ideas about intellectual potential influenced the statements about language and promulgated weird
conclusions: the vocabulary of a woman is smaller; male
language is more constructive, useful, and abstract; male
language has more complex, embedded constructions, while
female language is simple-minded with much emotional emphasis. It should be remembered here that these distorted
and stereotyped judgments were not restricted to sex differences. Varieties of languages had not yet been studied scientifically and the anthropologically- and sociologically-ori-
ented recognition of differences, without value judgments of
good/bad and normal/peculiar, was only beginning to be
established in the study of human beings and their behavior.

When Sapir published his study of abnormal speech
types of the Nootka language in 1915, he included fat people,
dwarfs, hunchbacks, lame people, left-handed people, cir-
cumcised males, cowards, baby talk, and women's speech.

No one questioned that some of these categories are not abnormal. (I have to admit that I didn't immediately see the
incongruity of including women's speech in abnormal types!)
An enlightened awareness will challenge that kind of classification. Analogous to this is a recent study on mental health
that showed double standards being applied in judging for male
and female what is normal, healthy behavior. [11] This ori-
entation of looking at language variation as different cultural
and sociological types, and the development of linguistics in
its maturing stages has led to the establishing of a sub-
discipline in linguistics called sociolinguistics. This branch
of linguistics studies the infinite varieties of language within
language: age differences, cultural differences, occupational
vocabulary, slang, styles of speech and writing, and many
others, but including, of course, sex differences in language.
Before the development of sociolinguistics, linguists were not
truly ready to talk about male/female differences because
none of these differences operates alone and without intri-
cate connections to other variables. The little girl rolling
her eyes and inveigling an ice cream cone from a tall adult
male, is indeed, using female language, but she is also using pre-school language; familial language (he is her father);
and dramatic language (the scene occurs in public). Now
that linguists are more sophisticated in methodology and
evaluations, we can look forward to enlightened language descriptions in the future.

Besides these obvious state-of-the-art reasons that we
do not have much information on actual male/female differences
in language, there are other realisms we have to face. Scientists are human beings and they sometimes bury ideas they
cannot cope with. A case in point is the study of sex origin
and development in the fetus. Recent information leads to
the conclusion that all human fetuses are originally female
but that upon some of them an active organizer substance
called androgen operates to cause the development of a male. [12]
In fact, a rather good case could be made that mankind's
first speech, "Madam, I'm Adam," is, indeed backwards, in
more ways than are apparent at the surface structure. [13] I
will refer to this again when the matter of gender/sex analysis
is discussed under linguistic structures.

Another area that is difficult or impossible to cope
with is the collection of discomforting vocabularies in linguistic behavior. A real investigation of the linguistic behavior
of male and female would treat areas of tyranny, discrimination and power displays, and involve some usage which is very
distasteful to certain people. One has to have a pretty strong

stomach to read through the vocabulary collected on females
as sex objects. [14] It would appear that philologists and
linguists through the years, keen enough to have observed
these offensive distinctions, might have avoided further investigation as an area they could not cope with for the same
reasons that prison language had not been documented in
earlier years. A further difficulty in research and understanding of the phenomenon of human behavior is the climate
of the society around the research institutions. The other
day on the radio a news commentator spoke about the recently
published love letters of Winston Churchill. He was extolling
the life-long love affair of the Churchills, but lamented that,
among other things, the rivalry between male and female
today is destroying the beautiful love relationships of male
and female! This kind of distorted logic fortifies and per-
petuates the myths and scares off timid researchers. What
isn't recognized in that kind of sentimental propaganda is
that it is the myths/misconceptions and untruths that separate
male and female and inhibit communion and understanding.

Human beings are always interested in explanations of
the phenomena that exist and move around us. From the
time youngsters learn to speak, they start asking, "Why?"
Scientists continue the tradition and work to find theoretical
explanations for the data they observe. Explanations for
sex roles are glibly passed off as child bearing or at least
related to child bearing and nurturing. Linguistic differences
are not so easily explained away by innate sexual differences.
That is, linguistic differences cannot be explained as physiological. There are perhaps some differences in the brain
which are not yet understood (I shall discuss this later).
The only physiological difference in the actual speech apparatus
is the size and length of the vocal folds (vocal cords), which
control pitch and quality of voice. This does not account for
the fact that some women speak lower than some men and
male/female linguistic behavior can still be distinguished.
Most of the differences noted have to do with vocabulary choice
and grammatical devices, neither of which has anything to do
with the physiology of speech mechanisms. One phonetician [15]
found in his studies of the vocal apparatus a performance behavior that remains curiously unexplained. More men than
women can roll up the edges of the tongue! This articulatory
virtuosity, however, never occurs in language sounds, and
one might conclude that the advantages are dubious, since
there doesn't seem to be much demand for people who can
curl up the edges of the tongue. If, then, the physiological
differences are minimal, why are the culturally learned

differences so ubiquitous? Scholars have attempted to explain
"women's language" in various ways, such as historical,
sociological, psychological, and religious. Sir James Frazer,
at the beginning of this century, attempted to explain the
origin of gender in language. Kraus, a psychoanalyst, spent
considerable effort in compiling the hypotheses of various
writers up to 1924 concerning the phenomena of male/female
differences in languages. Then she proceeds, as expected
out of Vienna, to give the real reason!--the psychoanalytic
explanation. Royen later criticized Freud for his exaggerated
sexualistic doctrines in relation to the science of language. [16]
Probably, most of the differences can be explained on the
basis of role expectancies and beliefs (myths?) of society:
Man Does, Woman Is. [17] Throughout the millenia women
have accepted this with the dignity of futility.

In truth, explanations must go far beyond our present
imaginations into the beginnings of relationships between
human beings. People have had to eat to survive. Hunting
at times took the males away from the camp fire and the
family circle--however that family might have been consti-
tuted at that time. Hunting language would soon have been
distinguished as one aspect, and a male one, of the material
culture of the people. After a time it would result that the
entire economic system of the society would similarly find
its own language. Thus, economics in language would have
been an early important association. Whatever was barter-
able was the precursor of money, in itself a special kind of
communication. The exchange of goods soon incorporated
females and all of this involvement of economics, kinship
and marriage, and communication or language is undoubtedly
the foundation of other varieties in language based on status
and sex. [18] It is significant that a recent book on marriage
is entitled Pigs, Pearlshells, and Women. [19] Robert Graves
succinctly observed: "Marriage, like money, is still with
us; and, like money, progressively devalued. The ties between these two male inventions get closer and closer." [20]
George Bernard Shaw also commented on the "commercial
interpretation of marriage" and, further, noted that a "marked
difference is made in price between a new article and a sec-
ondhand one"--the "damaged goods" syndrome. [21] This is
paralleled in linguistic terms for women who are not virgins.

While the development of economics and all that is
entailed was essential for the survival of the human race,
supernatural or religious beliefs quickly followed. Basic
distinctions in belief systems have to do with living and non-

living beings and things, and their interdependency. At this
point it looks simple enough--we think we know what is living
and what isn't. But it is not that easy; societies--and lan-
uages--classify the parts of the world differently. Most of
the time they overlap, but it is the grey areas of non-agree-
ment in the thinking of human beings which cause us to pon-
der. For example, a moldy fungus would be a living organ-
ism to a scientist, but not to a rubber hunter in the Amazon
jungle. However, the large tree standing near the third bend
of the river is a supernatural "living" being to the rubber-
hunter, but is not a living being to many sophisticated scientists. Male human beings have souls, but, variously--depending
upon the group making the judgment--tables, giraffes, Indians,
trees, pets, fetuses, insects, and women <u>don't</u> have souls.
Thus, <u>categories</u> are supremely important in controlling the
behavior of <u>human</u> beings. In subtle, at times almost im-
perceptible ways, classificatory systems correlate with language structures and control the syntax of language as they
control other behavior of people. In languages, there is a
very close relationship between genders and animate/inanimate
distinctions. Compare the two diagrams presented here.

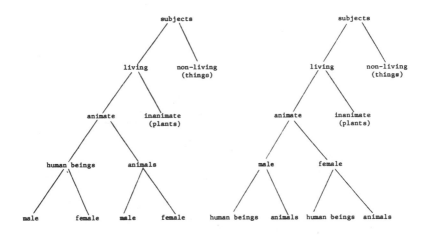

Which represents more closely the facts of the universe?
Which is the more basic category: human-beings/animals
or male/female? It should be noted that these diagrams
are not necessarily correct for all languages. They are
based on English categories and language. [22]

  To show how these concepts can be completely mis-
understood even by highly intelligent people, I quote a re-

nowned scholar of the last century. In discussing the Arawak
language of Guiana, he noted two genders, which he called
masculine and neuter. This kind of linguistic gender classification has nothing to do with diminishing females. Nevertheless, he mistakenly observed:

> A peculiarity ... is that [Arawak] only has two
> genders ... masculine and neuter. Man or nothing
> was the motto of these barbarians. Regarded as
> an index of their mental and social condition, this
> is an ominous fact. It hints how utterly destitute
> they are of those high, chivalric feelings, which
> with us centre around women. [23]

All of the Indo-European languages except Armenian
and Persian have masculine and feminine grammatical categories of gender in their linguistic systems. In some, as
we will see later, the gender system is very predominant--
every tree, table, chair, and stone has either a masculine,
feminine, or neuter assigned to it. In others, such as English, the gender system is evident only in a few pronouns:
she and he, his and her. In order to grasp the significance
of gender-consciousness in our world view, it is useful to go
outside of the Indo-European languages and see how other
people and languages deal with gender. This also we will
discuss later, but here I want to deal with this aspect of language and the origins of human beings. The Aztec language
is a good example, because we know something of their ancient beliefs and it is a language which does not have masculine and feminine gender in the grammatical system. The
singular pronouns are: nejua, tejua, and yejua, meaning,
respectively, first person singular (or I), second person singular (you), and third person singular. [24] This last pronoun
cannot be translated into English. It may refer to "he, she,
or it. " I believe that this is relevant to the concepts which
the Aztecs devised for the explanation of their origins. [25]
They believed that the origin of the world and all human
beings was one single principle with a dual nature. This supreme being had a male and female countenance--a dual god
who conceived the universe, sustains it, and creates life.
This god had the regenerating ability of both male and female. This dual deity, Ometeotl, had two different aspects
of a single supreme being. Ome = "two" and teotl = "god. "
The dynamic essence of this divine being was the feminine
and masculine nature--a whole god.

Ometeotl dwelt in a place called Omeyocan: "the

mansion of duality, the source of generation and life, the
ultimate or metaphysical region, the primordial dwelling
place.... " This god is spoken of in the singular grammatical form. There is a plural form in Aztec, if the ancients
had wanted to use it, but they referred to this god in the
singular. At the same time this singular divine being is
described as having a partner, which means "equal" or "a
thing which fits or adjusts with some other thing" or "that
which improves a thing or makes it more complete. "

Besides the gender difficulty in rendering these ideas
into English, there is the difficulty of the multitudes of gods
being one god. Do we use "is" or "are"? Note that I have
not used either pronoun referent "he" or "she" so far, in
reference to this Aztec god. There is nothing in the Aztec
language to indicate which gender should be used, and there
is simply no way to translate this into English. Nevertheless it is significant that the eminent authorities who discuss
Aztec religion all use the pronoun "he" in the discussions.
There is no more reason to use the male referent than to
use "she. " We can substitute the female referent just as
correctly: "She is Queen, she is Lord, above the twelve
heavens ... she exercises power over all things. She is
Lord and she rules. " Also in the translations, the words
"wife" and "consort" are used to designate the counterpart,
the partner. Again, there is no word in English, unless we
use the term "Siamese twin" to refer to this single dual being. This Siamese twin god was referred to as in Tonan,
in Tota, Huehueteotl, "the Mother, the Father, the old god. "
In fact, this divine being had many titles:

> Thus the tlamatinime [the sages], anxious to give
> greater vitality and richness to their concept of
> the supreme being, gave [the god] many names,
> laying the foundation for a comprehensive vision
> of the dual and ubiquitous divinity. And they did
> this through 'flower and song. '[26]

Thus, attempts at explanations and theoretical discussions continue--and will continue as long as human beings
like to talk with each other and ask questions. In reality,
what we must deal with now, whether or not we know the
explanation, is that for whatever the reasons, male and female linguistic behavior differs one from the other. In the
atmosphere of today's thinking in terms of Human Liberation,
surely the greatest and most profound of all revolutions, we
are even now witnessing linguistic change of male and female
behavior.

Chapter II

SOCIAL STRUCTURES:
MASCULINITY AND FEMININITY

There are many beliefs in human societies which are
accepted as facts even though there may be no proofs to sub-
stantiate the arguments. The beliefs about masculinity and
femininity are as fascinating as they are confusing, and there
is probably no area in the study of human behavior that is
more fraught with myths and superstitions, and unproved "conclusions." Even so, "masculinity" and femininity" are behavioral constructs which are powerful regulators of human
affairs.

Margaret Mead's classic studies on the male and female are basic for any attempts at understanding the social
structures of "masculinity" and "femininity." There are
widespread beliefs in our own society that certain attributes
of male and female are based on physiological differences,
and yet few of the so-called scientific studies can hold up to
careful scrutiny that considers the complex variables of learned
behavior. It is not easy to set up experiments to learn
about human behavior, for ethical reasons as well as for the
difficulties of learned interference and distracting variables.
Although the study of animal behavior has added an enormous
amount of information about living beings, it can be treach-
erous when its findings are extrapolated wholesale to human
beings. After a point, comparisons between animals and
humans are simply not valid. For example, the employment
of birth control among humans makes the matter of male/fe-
male behavior hardly comparable with that of other animals in
dealing with sex differences. Those who advocate that human
male dominance is in the "natural" order of things, often cite
examples from the chimpanzee community but regrettably,
they fail to complete the picture: the female chimpanzee,
when she is "in the pink," is capable of attracting males from
far and near. She apportions her pleasures with uninhibited
generosity. [27] How many human males would stand by and
share their wives with all the males in the neighborhood? Comparison of human and animal behavior must be done judiciously.

THE ALUMNAE

"Are you the house person who advertised for a
cleaning person?"

By Mary Gauerke; copyright ⓒ 1973 by The Register
and Tribune Syndicate; reproduced by permission.

There are, indeed, certain basic physical differences
between men and women which are accepted among scientists without contradiction.   Some of these will include:

(a) Females have less muscle and more fat.
(b) Females have less muscular strength.
(c) Females weigh less.
(d) Females tend to be less well coordinated, except
for fine hand movement.
(e) Females mature physically more rapidly.
(f) Females live longer. 28

These differences are acknowledged when convenient. Insur-
ance companies charge different rates on the basis of the longer life of females.   But these differences are not acknowledged
when role stereotypes are to be perpetuated. The medical profession does not seek out women to be surgeons and dentists,
even though female ability in fine hand movement exceeds the
male's. No one has suggested that women be put in charge of
the office of Secretary of State, even though we hear suggestions these days that aggressive behavior is an innate male
characteristic.   The fact that more males stutter doesn't keep
males from making speeches.

In investigating physiological differences, the brain is

one central area of interest with regard to male/female differences. Here we look for patterns that emerge with regard to
language or communication, since the brain is the seat of the
origins of language. It is said that the acquisition of one's own
native language is a human counterpart to imprinting in animals,[29]
as is the acquisition of a gender role and psychosexual identity.
We will see later that the sex differences in learned behavior begin very early in language. Are there differences in innate capacity? One scientist who has made recent discoveries about
the brain has encountered sex differences:

> In right-hemisphere tasks males tend to have a great-
> er left-visual-field superiority for dot location and
> dot enumeration than females. We also know that
> males are superior to females in certain visual-spa-
> tial tasks. It may be that right-hemisphere specializa-
> tion is more pronounced in males than in females....
>   In contrast, females tend to have greater verbal
> fluency than males. There is no evidence, however,
> that adult females are more asymmetrical in speech
> lateralization than males. Dichotic studies nonethe-
> less suggest that speech lateralization may develop
> earlier in girls than in boys. It appears that for some
> intellectual functions the brains of males and females
> may be differently organized. Most of human evolu-
> tion must have taken place under conditions where for
> the male hunting members of society accurate infor-
> mation about both the immediate and the distant en-
> vironment was of paramount importance. For the
> females, who presumably stayed closer to home with
> other nonhunting members of the group, similar se-
> lection processes may not have operated. It will be
> interesting to discover whether or not the sex differ-
> ences in verbal and nonverbal asymmetries we have
> uncovered with our relatively simple techniques hold
> true for other cultures.[30]

We need to know more about the physiological differences of the
brain of male and female in order to understand how the different sex patterns are "set" into the thinking and behavior of human beings in such pervasive and irreversible ways.

Even assuming that there are, in fact, basic physical
differences between males and females, it is immediately evident
that these differences do not apply equally to all males and females.
Some females have more muscle than some males. Some females
weigh more than some males, and some males have finer hand

movement than some females. We could chart the extremes
and the over-lapping on a scale:

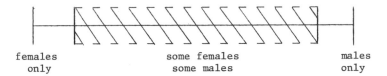

females   some females   males
  only   some males   only

Considering, then, the "all or none" and "some" variations
of human behavior, one has to come to the conclusion that
classifying occupations and behavior on sexual distinctions
has little relevance to the realities of life. The only appli-
cation that can be made of this scale to society is the use
of the "only" designated areas of difference. Such functions
as child-bearing and acting as wet nurse will never be performed by males. These concepts can be handled better as
a continuum rather than as a dichotomy.

    Different cultures handle these physical differences
in different ways. In our culture the males will carry heavy
packages, whereas in a hunting culture, the male must be
free to use the bow and arrow when a game animal is sud-
denly seen, and so the females carry the heavy packages.
In our culture the female precedes the male in a single-file
walking pattern; in the jungle cultures, the male, larger and
more muscular, precedes the female for very practical reasons: he has to be alert to danger and protect the smaller
persons. In a society such as ours where mechanization
and technology have superseded pristine muscular activities,
our beliefs have lagged far behind our actual situation.

    The matter of psychological differences is infinitely
more complex and it is also these concepts which underlie
the beliefs about masculinity and femininity. One way to
evaluate these differences is to note what occurs in other
societies with regard to male and female roles. Without
exception all cultures recognize different roles for male and
female. It is significant, however, that the rules for this
role behavior differ from culture to culture. What is considered female behavior in one culture may be male behavior
in another.[31] In the Amazon rainforest, men make the
pottery in one village, and a few hours away by canoe, in
another village, the women make the pottery. In western

cultures, the females knit, but in the Andes the males are
seen knitting as they walk along the stone-laid roads of the
incomparable Inca Empire.   In the near east, men cry without shame and are expected to express their emotions in this
way.   Men of western cultures are not permitted this outlet.
Sir Walter Scott summed it up:

> A child will weep at a bramble's smart,
> A maid to see her sparrow part,
> A stripling for a woman's heart;
> But woe awaits a country when
> She sees the tears of bearded men.

In our society, the psychological characteristics of
males are said to be: aggressive, assertive, authoritative,
competitive, courageous, daring, decisive, domineering, independent, innovative, self-reliant, vigorous, as well as
blunt, boastful, bull-headed, combative, presumptuous, pug-
nacious, sadistic and violent.   Females are said to be af-
fectionate, demure, dependent, emotional, excitable, gentle,
illogical, indecisive, intuitive, passive, sensitive, submissive, tender, unambitious, as well as bitchy, fickle, sac-
charine, secretive, superficial, undependable, vacillating,
whiney, and wily.   A recent textbook in gynecology noted
that, "The traits that compose the core of the female personality are feminine narcissism, masochism and passivity."[32]

It is difficult to separate out those qualities that are
desirable in a human way from those qualities which are
negative and destructive to the development of both male and
female as a human being.   One gets mixed up with sex roles
interfering with one's thinking.   Likewise it is almost impossible, at this stage of our knowledge, to separate those differences which are actual.   Real and imputed differences will
have to be sorted out before the final verdict.   The ideas of
femininity and masculinity are based on very old beliefs that
were formulated to try and explain the world as it was known
to mankind then.   The principle of opposites underlies western history: energy and inertia, active and passive, heaven
and earth, Lord and flesh, with, of course, the male and
female identification pervading these polar concepts.   Our
scientific tradition is based on the paternal principle of potency and even today this attitude is reflected in theoretical
discussions:

> In view of the obstinate preoccupation of the human
> mind with the theme of the potent, active--I would

almost say masculine--principle, before and quite
apart from any science of dynamics (and also with
its opposite, the passive, persisting principle on
which it acts), it is difficult to imagine any science
in which there would not exist a conception of force
(and of its opposite, inertia).[33]

LaBarre artfully noted that western society became
burdened with false gender and that we falsely impute human
sexual dimorphism to nature. He went on to say,

...nature is itself, and is neither she nor he--
but a self-identity which we dichotomize as motion
or Energy (male) and substance or Mass (female)....
...man now knows that E quite demonstrably
and indubitably equals mc^2; i.e., matter and energy
are the same thing under a different guise, or the
same fundamental reality in a different phase or
state of being. [34]

Robert Graves, another sensitive observer of the female dilemma, also referred to the basic nature:

Goethe prophesied the eventual rejuvenation of our
world by a going-back to Nature. If, however, he
was right, 'Nature' must be interpreted not as
natura naturata, 'Nature as scientifically observed',
but as natura naturans, 'creative Nature', which
implies the power of love. Nor must love be read
as grand-scale international philanthropy; but as a
personal understanding between Barak, the male
mind, and Deborah, the female mind. This alone
can lift humanity out of the morass where intellectual arrogance has sunk it and develop the so-called
supernatural powers of which both sexes are capable. [35]

Our obsession with relegating almost everything to the
male/female dichotomy may have even influenced our interpretation of other philosophies. The Chinese principles of
yang and yin were originally conceived of forces that were
symbolized by light and dark, firm and yielding, positive
and negative. The ancient Chinese believed that the world
of being arises out of the change and interplay of these forces. As these ideas were translated into western societies,
masculinity and femininity were introduced. An early translator of the I Ching (or Book of Changes) notes that some of

these ideas are foreign to the original thought of the I Ching. [36]
Subsequently, western thinking added what it wanted, and even
uses the ideas to sell pop jewelry with the appeal: "Yin and
Yang pendants--Yin symbolizes femininity, darkness, coolness
... Yang is the symbol of virility, light, warmth."

It should be noted that the concepts of "masculinity"
and "femininity" do not occupy so much attention in other cultures and languages of the world. There are languages
where the terms do not occur, though all languages have
some way of indicating male and female. This is not to say
that there is less sexual activity in those societies; on the
contrary, a case might be made that sexual activity occurs
in inverse proportion to the amount of attention given to
masculinity and femininity in advertising and dialogue. In
the frenetic quest for femininity and masculinity in our society, both sexes project those qualities they admire and
desire on the opposite sex. In denying themselves the qualities which are said to belong to the opposite sex, people
glorify these qualities in the opposite sex out of proportion.
Men deny themselves sensitivity and gentleness, but desire
these qualities in their women. Women deny themselves
assertive and authoritative behavior, and demand these qualities of their men. If the partners can conform to these
stereotypes, then, well and good. But if the partners cannot sustain these ideals, then there is conflict, confusion,
and disappointment.

Today, the concepts of masculinity and femininity are
being challenged and in many cases are being rejected as
unworkable and destructive. Many people of this generation
don't know if they are men or women because they have rejected the definitions of previous millenia. There is growing recognition that not all people favor the life styles that
once were thought to be the only way, and that the "family"
is not necessarily composed of the much-cherished nuclear
structure, found in children's books and romantic tales, but
not necessarily in real life: father, mother, son, and daughter. People are re-evaluating what is "right" and "good" in
practical terms of what is real. Adjustments to new positions
must take place. For the human race to survive, males
will have to define themselves as less aggressive, and in
order for womenkind to lift themselves out of their depres-
sion, females will have to define themselves as more aggressive.

What has all this to do with language? Superficially,
perhaps nothing. In profound and basic ways, these concepts

underlie what it is thought proper for females to say and hear, and what it is thought possible for females to create, in the way of great literature and ideas.

Chapter III

SOCIAL DIALECT DIFFERENCES:
DIALOGUES AND STYLES OF SPEECH

Human beings all over the world, in every language,
have uncounted varieties of language to use in different social
and cultural situations. People have used and responded to
social differences since the beginning of time, but only recently have these varieties come to be studied in a scientific way
in a relatively new branch of linguistics called sociolinguistics.
This branch of study entails looking at various dimensions of
language use in various situations. There are, for example,
differences in language that are based on geographical dimensions. Southerners talk differently from northerners; people
in Great Britain talk differently from people in the United
States; Australians sound different from speakers of English
in South Africa. There are also differences based on tem-.
poral dimensions. Grandfathers talk differently from grand-
sons; people talked differently a century ago from the way
they do now. The language used three or four hundred years
ago when the King James Bible was translated and Shakespeare
wrote his plays is even a little difficult to understand today
because of the temporal dimensions. Going back another
two hundred years or so to the times when Chaucer wrote,
one finds the language even more difficult to understand.

Besides these spatial and temporal dimensions, there
is a highly complex array of social and cultural dimensions
that every human being has to learn from birth. There are
age and sex and status dimensions that are inherent in every
dialogue situation. There are language varieties as a result
of bilingual or other language influence. In California the
vocabulary is enriched by Spanish loan words such as tamale,
taco, and olla. In Pennsylvania one hears expressions and
folk songs influenced by the German language, "Throw Mama
from the train, a kiss, a kiss!" Occupational milieu certainly affects the use of language. Campus lingo is not always
understood by parents when the student returns home; the
space age added new expressions and vocabulary to the language. Surfers, tramps, beauticians, criminals, politicans,

30

By Reg Smythe; copyright © 1972 Daily Mirror Newspaper,
Ltd.; reproduced by permission of Publishers-Hall Syndicate.

---

and all groups of people have their own style of language
which shows who is "in" and who is not.

    In addition to these many varieties of use of language,
there are other conditions which influence the choice of forms
and vocabulary.   Following an old scholar from another century, I am calling this the context of situation. [37] It comprises, briefly, the how, when, and where, the who with,
the what, and under what circumstances.   The choice of the

variety of language depends on how the communication is to
be conveyed: by telephone, by signals, or by shouting.
When the message is produced also dictates the choice: before breakfast or after.   Further, where the participants are
located spatially--in the office, at the park, in a night club--
has an influence.   The description and relationship of the
speaker-hearer determines the expressions used and the non-
participants, or the audience, affect language behavior.   The
physical condition of the surroundings, that is, the amount
of light, noise, silence, and artifacts change the language
behavior.   The mood of the society itself subtly permits and
prohibits certain language forms.   Individual behavior and
condition of health make their impact on the use of language
in the dialogue.   With all of these complexities implicit in
language behavior, it is a miracle that human beings understand each other at all.

After some thought and study about language, one sees
that none of these situations can occur without involvement
from other dimensions.   Wrong conclusions can be drawn
without considering all of these factors in the discussions of
human language.   Specifically, it would be a mistake to try
to consider male/female language in isolation from the matrix
in which it functions.   As an illustration of the many varieties,
consider the different ways one might make an invitation for
lunch.   For a business acquaintance: "Mrs. Smith would
like to invite you and Mrs. Jones to lunch next week."   To
one's parents: "Say, folks, can you come on up for lunch
next week?"   To a friend of the same sex: "How about let's
meet for lunch next week?"   To one's children: "Get in here
for lunch now!"   To a foreigner: "Would you be free to join
us for lunch next week?"   To a potential sex partner: "Well,
ummm, I was just wondering ... could you come over for a
little lunch this week-end?"

Changes in society cause certain behavioral patterns
to come under the light of scrutiny.   When society is ex-
periencing earthquakes of change, it is tempting to make statements and draw conclusions which are distorted and out of
focus.   Thus, when a social awareness points to the poor, or
to black people, or to women, or to criminals, or to Com-
munists, it is inevitable that these groups, which may have
long been out of focus and in an unbalanced relationship, now
become spotlighted out of proportion.   We must constantly
remind ourselves that we must not look at male/female behavior in isolation.

Doing so leads to hysterical and extreme observations.

For example, recently I came across a statement about the
Aztec language [38] in a women's liberation journal. It said,
in effect, that in the Aztec language "to take a prisoner,"
"to bear a child," "to be sacrificed as a prisoner," and "to
die in childbed" are the same word. [39] The implications are
horrendous! It caught my attention because my first linguistic
experiences were with the modern Aztec language in Mexico
and consequently I knew many Aztec families. I had never
received the impression that Aztec mothers ever had the
feeling they were being sacrificed as prisoners. In calmer
retrospect, one can find a more rational, scholarly explanation of the Aztec situation that led to this wrong conclusion.
In the old Aztec religion there were several heavens, or
after-abodes for departed souls. The most elevated and honored heaven with the highest rank and most pleasant circumstances was reserved for men who died in battle, prisoners
who were sacrificed to the gods, and women who died in childbirth. This most glorious of all heavens was a happy pros-
pect and instilled courage into the hearts of soldiers and
women facing peril in childbirth. [40]

The misinterpretation and misunderstanding of this
Aztec belief is possible when the customs and words are
lifted out of context. Because the study of male/female behavior patterns has the potential of highly emotionally charged
reactions, it is absolutely necessary to keep the discussions
integrated in an overall concept of human linguistic and other
behavior. In examining the vocabulary and styles of speech
in dialogue and conversation, one must note (1) the sex of
the speaker, (2) the sex of the hearer, (3) the sex of the
person referred to or spoken of, and (4) the sexes of the
audience. The forms of language used and the vocabulary
permitted and prohibited have to do with the answers to these
questions.

One way to look at general usage in language is to
think of a continuum with rather mild, unobtrusive items on
one end and ranging toward strong, trauma-producing expressions at the other end. The extremes of the continuum are
correlated with male and female usage. The chart on the
next page illustrates this.

Vocabulary items and expressions which illustrate
the "feminine" usage on the left side of the chart are such
items as: "precious, cute, teeny, abdomen, Oh dear! How
perfectly sweet!" The continuum moves toward strong or
brutish terms, such as "belly" or "guts" and finally to ob-

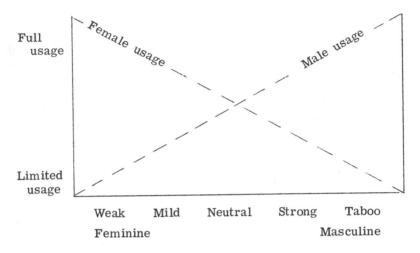

scenities and items which, until recently, rarely found their
way into print. If males use language as that defined on the
left side of the chart, they are thought to be effeminate; if
females use language as that defined on the right side of the
chart, they are thought to be coarse. The refreshingly honest
use of language by former President Harry Truman was consonant with his character, and he sometimes disregarded the
proprieties and exploded his "male usage" in public. The
story is told of a conversation of his once with a group of
farmers, when he continually used the word "manure." This
sounded a bit stilted to one of the audience, who pleaded with
his wife, Bess, to get him to say "fertilizer." Patient Bess
refused, for, she said, "It's taken me 30 years to get him
to say 'manure'!"

       Another perspective is offered in the matter of vocabu-
lary domains which show male/female patterns. Language
and culture are two inseparable components in the lives of
human beings. The roles of male and female define certain
areas where participation is exclusive of the other sex. Lexical domains are reflections of interests and roles and are
learned behavior. The domains of women traditionally have
been childbirth and rearing, colors, cooking, and sewing.
The domains of men traditionally have been machinery, politics, and war. Note that these are not exclusive. Today as
never before we see a crossing over and exchange of domains
as roles merge and modify along with varying behavior. The
male interior decorator has more vocabulary versatility in
colors and fabrics than most females. The male gourmet cook

is well-versed in cooking terminology.   The female engineer
and chemist can handle the technical terms of those domains
as well as the males in the profession.   The male obstetri-
cian has a larger vocabulary in the domain of childbirth than
mothers.   The female head of state is conversant in the language of politics and war.   Note the difference between linguistic constraints that grammatical rules allow or don't allow,
and these co-occurrences that are reflections of socio-cultural
structures.

Beyond the consideration of vocabulary permitted, there
are all sorts of possibilities of attitudes which can be conveyed
by choice of vocabulary.   An example is seen in the attitude
toward moonshine whiskey, in the mountain speech of male
and female.   The women refer to this 'evil' as "that old
whuskey" and the men refer to that which provides a pleasurable pastime as "liquor."[41]   The set of interjections which
male and female use range from dear and precious items
such as those found on the left side of the chart to swear
words on the right.

The study of conversations or dialogue with regard to
male and female participation often reflects the regard which
males in our society have for the intelligence and thoughtful
intellectual contribution of females.   Jonathan Swift, a keen
observer of communication on many levels, appreciated the
conversation of women immensely, and confessed that he even
left the company of men after one dinner party to join the
ladies, because, he said, the discourse of the men "degen-
erated into smart Sayings of their own Invention...."   In his
essays on conversation he attributed the degeneracy that affected the conversation of the period to "the Custom arisen,
for some Years past, of excluding Women from any Share in
our Society, farther than in Parties at Play, or Dancing, or
in the Pursuit of an Amour."[42]

In order to understand the dyadic relationship in conversation one might use the analogy of "antiphon" as found
in musical composition.   There are two voices to carry the
melodic line.   In a balanced antiphonal composition (or conversation), the two voices carry equal responsibility for the
melody (or message).   One musical idea is expressed (a sentence) and then it is answered by another musical idea.   Observation of dialogues with male and female participants very
often shows there is not an equal amount of participation with
each carrying his and her share of the melodic line.   Rather,
in most cases the males dominate the melodic line, stopping

here and there for the accompanying female voices to fill in,
ask questions, give assurance, and, in all, to keep the men going. If a woman tries to add some melody (or idea) of her
own, often the man's head turns away, or he interrupts (not
having heard her) and continues his own theme. The woman's
part, then, in many acts of male/female conversation, is to
make coffee and further the conversation of men.

D. H. Lawrence, a master at reducing spoken language
to written language, was aware of this imbalance. In Lady
Chatterley's Lover, Connie spent much energy entertaining
the many male guests of her husband. Evenings were spent
in conversation between the men.

> Silence fell. The four men smoked. And Connie
> sat there and put another stitch in her sewing....
> Yes, she sat there! She had to sit mum. She
> had to be quiet as a mouse, not to interfere with
> the immensely important speculations of these highly-
> mental gentlemen. But she had to be there. They
> didn't get on so well without her; their ideas didn't
> flow so freely.

After several pages of dialogue, Connie finally speaks:

> 'There are nice women in the world,' said Connie,
> lifting her head up and speaking at last.
> The men resented it.... she should have pre-
> tended to hear nothing. They hated her admitting
> she had attended so closely to such talk. [43]

Through the centuries women have listened silently to the
men-folk talk. Men do not sit quietly and listen to women
talk.

Styles of speech are many and varied throughout conversations. Again, male/female patterns are evident. Baby
talk is a style of speech which is used to show a certain relationship or to control another human being. Both male and
female use baby talk, but since it is not usual to use this
style in public, there is little documentation on actual use.
Baby talk also occurs in other languages [44] and in general
it appears that it is a style of speech which females use more
frequently than males. Mothers may use it to sons longer than
to their daughters. Males may use it to their car, or their
gun--or when they are drunk. Fathers may use it to their
small children, "Is 'er Daddy's 'ittle dirl?"

A style of speech which we can simply call <u>patronizing</u> is often heard when those spoken to are children, foreigners, inferiors, the mentally incompetent, hospitalized patients, or females. On radio talk shows, for example, one can often hear this kind of language used with callers, particularly with women. Male newscasters have some difficulty in relating to other newscasters who are <u>not</u> male. On a recent news program the anchorman introduced the next newscaster as"... lovely Jane Doe. " On another program, after the female reporter completed her part, the anchorman acknowledged it with, "Thank you, dear!" One would not use this tone of voice and style of speech to a professional colleague. Another type of speaking, employed by males to females, is the language of <u>explanations.</u> Males are forever explaining things to women. It is rare that a male will have the patience or desire to listen to explanations from females. Males are the givers of information, not the receivers. The male who uses <u>explanation</u> is not really interested in the female's acquiring more knowledge. (Heaven forbid!) Rather, he is showing his superiority.

The <u>language of apology</u> belongs predominantly to the female. Women are always being sorry or asking pardon for something. Whether or not they are to blame for something is not the issue. Men also say, "I'm sorry" or "Excuse me" occasionally, but it is a way of life for females. This is undoubtedly related to the submissive gestures and smiling of the female which will be discussed further in the chapter on nonverbal behavior. Female language demonstrates greater use of <u>hyperbole,</u> accompanied by strong emphasis patterns: "I'd just <u>die</u>!" "He'll <u>never</u> forgive me!" "It was the most <u>extraordinary</u> hat!" The "cackling hens" effect of women's higher voices and rhythms was superbly stylized in a voice choir performance in <u>The Music Man.</u> In actual practice, when males and females are carrying out their professional or business roles, the style of language is usually much the same. The skillful use of occupational language, at this point, is a higher and more encompassing requirement than maintenance of sex-role language.

There is the matter in everyone's life of changing roles, and changing clothes, and for our discussion, changing styles of language to suit the situation. The "tell it like it is" atmosphere of today has fostered the idea that language used in one situation ought to be used in all. There is the fallacy of hypocrisy that believes it is wrong to change styles of language for different situations. Actually it is not any more

hypocritical to choose to wear a bathing suit at the beach and
a business suit at the office, than it is to use sexy langauge
in a sex scene and occupational language at work.   As a matter of fact, women must learn other styles of language, as
they assume other styles of living.

People are judged by language.   You can dress in an
indeterminate way, but once you open your mouth to speak,
you have stated who you are and what you want.   Remember
My Fair Lady.   Therefore women will continue to be judged
as trite, unauthoritative, dull, insipid, and uninteresting, if
they continue to talk that way.   Those who insist on sex dichotomy in language use are doomed to limitations and restrictions that are antithetical to creativity.   They will be
isolated from growth and freedom.

Chapter IV

GINGERBREAD MEN AND GINGERBREAD GIRLS:
LABELS AND DESCRIPTORS

It is a commonplace that labels and words which are
used to refer to people and to describe others are based on
deep-seated attitudes toward those particular people or groups
of persons. It is also true, however, that these basic and
underlying attitudes are not often acknowledged, or even recognized. It is very difficult, for example, for anyone to explain satisfactorily the difference between "lady" and "woman."
Yet these terms are used among the population in very orderly
and systematic patterns that express attitudes toward females
or toward a particular female. The difference, perhaps, can
be illustrated by two expressions: "The women, God help
us!" and "The ladies, God bless them!"[45] "Lady" is decep-
tively used, at times, as a form of flattery, supposedly to
exalt the person and lift her above the ordinary. Every
woman has been told at some time in her life that she shouldn't
want to be equal with men because she is already superior!
In fact, the result is to put her aside on the pedestal and
not have to deal with her. Business and government cannot
be run by committees and executive positions staffed with
pedestal-ladies. These jobs have to be done by people whose
feet are on the ground!

The etymology, or the history of the meanings of a
word, is sometimes, and wrongly, used to control the dimensions of conduct permitted persons referred to by that word.
For example, the origin of "woman" goes back to "wifman"
or "wife-man"--pointing toward the belief that a woman has
no being apart from a husband. Sometimes we refer to the
past to try to justify our own beliefs. Quite apart from being unfair, this use of the history of words is linguistically
unsound. The word "silly," for example, used to have a
meaning "blessed," and still does in some cases in German.
Today, in English, however, it would be difficult to foist the
concept of blessedness on a silly fool! Likewise, to try to
bring the meanings of long-ago into the words, "woman"

"PRESIDENTPERSON, CHAIRPERSON, HONORED GUESTPERSONS AND PERSONPERSONS..."

---

or "lady" or "mistress, " and direct the status of females based upon those meanings, even though historically of interest, is nonsensical.   Over-enthusiasts even create fictitious etymologies.   It is said that Ruskin often reminded the married women. in his audiences that their place was in the home because "wife" meant "she who weaves. "[46] Not so.   But even if it were, the original meaning of "lady" was "bread-kneader. " Would Ruskin send the ladies back to kneading dough?

When the labels for male and female are paired, we see other social structures exemplified.   The couplet "man and wife" instead of "husband and wife" suggests that her existence is in relationship to the man and implies a subordinate position-- the "Other" which Simone de Beauvoir speaks of. [47]   The words "man" and "woman" have their counterparts "master" and "mistress" but the respective meanings of these pairs are vastly different.   A woman's master is nothing like a man's mistress!   One can be effeminate, but one cannot be emasculate.   We know what a ladies' man is, but who has heard of a gentlemen's woman?

Some words have as yet no counterpart.   The term "housewife" has stood alone for centuries with no "househusband. "   Lately I saw the term "house-husband" in an article that had to do with shopping for nourishing food.   This makes sense when one notes the growing number of male shoppers in the supermarket.   The word "housewife" is often used

with modifiers which must be considered in the total meaning
of the term.   Recently, in the letters to the editor column
of a newspaper, a writer referred to herself as: "a young
housewife," "a dumb housewife," and "just a housewife." If
the English language begins to embrace the concept and term
for "house-husband," it is likely that these modifying elements
will change to something like a hypothetical: "a vigorous
house-husband/wife," or "an intelligent house-husband/wife,"
or "a distinguished house-husband/wife." That kind of language change will come with social change.

The counterparts in couplets can also designate distinct status relationships.   In the military, where status is
a well-defined concept by rank, one refers to "officers and
their ladies" and "enlisted men and their wives." Linguistic
labels in the matter of marital status reflect the attitudes of
society toward male and female. A previously married man
is a "bachelor"; a previously married woman is a "divorcée,"
with the implications being that a bachelor has a future, and
a divorcée has had a past.

A baffling lack in the matter of labels is that there is
no way for persons "over thirty" to refer to their constant
companion of the opposite sex.   "Boyfriend" or "girlfriend"
sounds so teen-agish and "lover" doesn't seem to be a dis-
creet way to talk about someone in a general context.   Language again reflects the Puritanical tradition of obliterating
any possible male/female relationship except man and wife.
Another lack in English that is devastating and inhibiting is
the deficiency in our language for warm and respectable terms
to refer to the sex act. [48]   How pathetic it is that the only
way we can discuss this function is to use scientific Latin
words or "obscenities."   Other languages are richer in their
paradigms for making love.

Adult females often are labeled "girl" and "baby" even
though they may be perfectly responsible members of society.
Only recently a newscaster announced that "a California girl"
had assumed command of the WAVES.   This officer had the
rank of Commander, a very distinguished rank in the Navy,
and was later promoted to Captain.   The parallel construction is conspicuously absent: "A California boy just assumed
the position of Secretary of HEW."

Labels for females range from these mild forms which
reflect social structures to insulting terms which reflect individual attitudes. In a society which claims to have the highest

regard for women in the Christian tradition, it is indeed shocking to discover that our state and government leaders can still
use offensive vocabulary in reference to females in public offices.   A generation ago an important dictionary maker noted
that "Over the years many terms for the word <u>woman</u> have
become degraded."[49] Apparently discrimination against women
is still socially acceptable.   Two illustrations will suffice.
In a discussion of committees during the last national election,
one of our U. S. senators prescribed that no women would
be permitted on a certain committee.   He simply declared,
"No broads!" and would discuss the issue no more.   This
is analogous to using such words as "wop, greaser, hunky,
coon, or nigger" but almost no public official would dare use
those words these days.   This acceptance of insulting language
can go to the extreme.   Recently the trash barrels at the
California Institution for Men, a corrective place, were painted
with the silhouette of a woman, with a girl's name, and the
words, "Use me."   One of the barrels had a silhouette that
was obviously pregnant, with the accompanying words, "I've
been used."   A complaint was made to the official in charge
that this was inappropriate in a public institution using tax
funds, but he defended the practice as "simply a take-off on
current advertising of a well-known airline."   Only when extensive pressure was brought to bear were the barrels re-
painted.

     It should be pointed out here that these examples are
not drawn from a limited and special segment of the population.   These were not high criminals negotiating in a back
room, nor trash containers in an off-beat bawdy house; rather
these examples concern tax-supported public offices.   The
most notable thing about such linguistic behavior is how widely
it is tolerated.   Does this say something about masochistic/
sadistic tendencies in human beings?   Do human beings need
to insult and to be insulted to survive?

     Bias in the language eventually gets caught in the trap
of the ludicrous or the incongruous.   A book advertisement
said that Elizabeth I matured into a "true prince."   Pearl
Bailey and Hazel Kohring each received a "Man of the Year"
award.   A female opera singer who had a great voice was
called a "Caruso in petticoats."   And we learn that "men-
strual pain accounts for an enormous loss of man-hours of
work."   The column "Men and Events" often has newsworthy
items about females.   One can be appalled at the unthinking,
uncreative, and limited use of language in these instances.

     A study of the <u>descriptions</u> of females who are in public

or professional positions provides other examples of the actual
values put on females in society.   The following are illustrations I have collected from magazines and newspapers.   The
women described are not women who won the lottery, but are
women who have positions entailing a good deal of training
and expertise.   The women were variously described as: "a
serene, delicately formed woman" (referring to an executive
chairperson); "a brown-eyed cutie" (referring to an athlete);
"(she) speaks softly ... blushes and laughs..." (referring to
a commanding officer); "a very feminine woman" (referring
to a chief of a Flight Service Station).   A pilot was headlined
as "Woman flier...."   A member of a commission was designated a "mother."   A book which received considerable attention was written by a "housewife with an Oxford degree in
English."   Apparently an attempt is being made to assure
women they can still remain sexually attractive even if pro-
fessionally competent.   I have not found similar examples for
males of equal professional status.   The focus on description for this caliber of occupation, one would expect, should
be on qualifications for the job--not physical or emotional attributes.   These illustrations indicate something of the im-
maturity of society in relating to females.

     Careful observation of all kinds of written materials
produces illustrations of prejudice which we all passed over
unthinkingly until recently: "A cry or a scream of a monkey,
like that produced by a frightened woman..."; "A woman from
the East Coast, nearly in tears..."; "[the accent or dialect]
of Kentucky and Tennessee ... its feminine shrillness...."
The honored and prestigious Encyclopaedia Britannica speaks,
in regard to Catherine of Aragon, of her "failure to produce
a male to the throne...."   It wasn't Henry's syphilis, but
Catherine's failure!   In a discussion of the development of
Pennsylvania, an historian says, "The new constitution ...
remedied all the injustices ... providing for equality of rep-
resentation ... and for universal male suffrage.   Pennsylvania
had now become a genuine democracy."[50]   An advertisement
to attract young women to a training program promised the
candidates that they would be trained in "qualities every man
seeks in a wife."   Bets were taken on the Miss World contest in London's gambling circles, and the bookmakers ad-
mitted that the talk about the "favorites" did make the girls
sound like racehorses.

     The matter of order is of concern to scientists who
study behavioral events.   There are hierarchies and values
seen in whether elements in the study come first or last,
or which come before others.   For example, in the wills

filed in the vital statistics, it was common practice in the
old days to list the children of the deceased with the sons
listed before the daughters, if the daughters were named at
all.   This precedent of order preference still holds in the
thinking of some people today.   During the recent presidential
campaign a popular magazine printed a picture of Eleanor and
George McGovern with their five children.

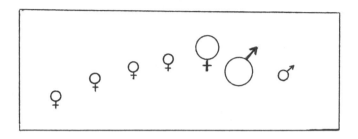

The seating position of the family by itself indicates no special relationships.   The caption under the picture, however,
lists the son first, and then returns to the left side of the
picture and lists the daughters.   This high value put on sons
is, of course, of very long standing.   Thomas Aquinas in-
structed his followers that in a fire, a man saves first his
sons, then his wife.

    The terminology which is used in labeling and des-
cribing members of society is a subtle (but sometimes not
so subtle) reflection of the structures of society in terms of
status, quality, permitted performance, and values.   For
hundreds and thousands of years human beings have used this
kind of language mostly without ever recognizing its discrimi-
natory impact and without challenging its continuance.   Only
recently, with the greater linguistic understanding of use of
language in all situations have these biased elements come
into focus in observing male and female linguistic behavior.

Chapter V

TITLES, NAMES, AND GREETINGS

When I was on a research trip in the southern region
of the United States during the late 1960s I met a young man
who caused me to think more seriously about titles, which
was apropos of the South, where titles of all kinds are used
more than in other places in the United States.   The "Colo-
nels" and the "Captains" abound.   I had stopped to get gaso-
line and used my identification and credit cards which have
the "Dr." title.   The young man attending queried me on it,
and added, with a mixture of awe and admiration, "Gawrsh,
I've never seen a <u>woman</u> doctor!"   He then insisted that I
receive as a gift for accomplishment one of the watermelons
he had been selling.   The charm and candid appreciation,
however, were somewhat dimmed as I drove off in contem-
plation.   In the twentieth century, in an "enlightened" nation
where all females are "equally" educated, a professional woman is still a rarity or an oddity.

Those who study human behavior have observed that
titles of address, use of proper names, and greetings reveal
something of the structure of the community in question.[51]
The use of these means of identification has to do with the
role one is carrying out, the response desired, and the relationship between the speakers and the hearers.   Status relationships are signaled in very concrete ways by use of titles
and first and last names.   But before making particular judgments regarding the observed usage of these tags, one must
consider the more general use within the context.   Some institutions and organizations are more apt to use high-sounding
titles and names.   Nicknames would be avoided; "Dr." would
be preferred to "Mr."   In institutions of higher education, a
reverse snobbery sometimes takes place, where acquired
titles such as "Dr." are avoided and the more general "Mr.,"
"Mrs.," or "Miss" are preferred.   Use of titles also differs
according to geography.   In the South of the United States,
in Europe, and in Mexico, one is more likely to hear elabo-
rate use of titles.   In Germany, a professor carries three
titles: "Herr Professor Doktor" or "Frau Professor Doktor."

"I NOW PRONOUNCE YOU MAN AND MS."

The use of first names is not common in Europe and Latin American countries. It would be unheard of between strangers. In California, however, it is not unusual to hear a speaker address a stranger by the first name. When I was an advisor to international college students, I learned that these students had their own set of values in the use of first names. To a group from the Sudan, (who spoke excellent English), titles meant cold, formal distance. First names meant warmth and friendship.

In contrast, in the United States first names are often used to establish an inferior position for blacks. It was a matter of great adjustment to Americans who wanted to give these foreign black students proper respect by addressing them by their titles! In similar ways, male and female use of first and last names is delicate and difficult to interpret--especially in these days of changing habits.

The interchange of naming is done on a reciprocal or a nonreciprocal basis. This has to do with status relationships. Persons of equal status are more likely to use reciprocal naming--either they both use first names, or they both use titles and last names. When observing the use of titles between male and female and in male/female usage, it is of concern to note the reciprocal relationships. Do both parties exchange first names, or does one party use first name and

the other party use title and last name? It will be seen that
males use first names for females more often than females
use first names for males. This is not to do with sex or
femininity, but rather status distinctions. In these cases
males are in a higher position or a position of authority.
Even in marriage this nonreciprocal titling used to occur,
especially in the Victorian Era, when even in intimate situations many wives would address their husbands as "Mr.
Smith" or "Dr. Smith" instead of using his first name.

In recent times with the concepts of "equal status"
and "female status" being brutally examined, some bizarre
or at least interesting uses are being tried out in an attempt
to find a pattern of naming and titling both useful and respect-
ful to all concerned. Previously the Ph. D. title of a woman
was often ignored when her husband also had a Ph. D. For
example, one might have read, "This map was prepared by
Mrs. John Doe" rather than "by Prof. Jane Doe." Today a
great deal of experimentation is going on to find a comfortable way to address them both. "Drs. Jane and John Doe"
occurred recently in an advertisement for a book which husband and wife co-authored. Also observed are: Dr. John
and Dr. Jane Doe; Drs. John and Jane Doe; Dr. John Doe
and Dr. Jane Doe. And why not Drs. Jane Doe, if one doesn't
know his first name? Imagine the possibilities!

When women continue to function in traditional roles
there is no confusion in which title to use or how to address
them. With women assuming other roles in society, patterns
of behavior have not yet been established. I have received
mail with an endless variety of titles acknowledging my several roles, even such conglomerates as: "Dr. and Ms. and
Mrs. Mary Key" and Ms. Ph. D. Mary Key." Some of this
is out of humor, but I think based on a struggle to find better ways to relate to females' attainment which has been ignored before. Not all businesses have caught up to the times,
however, as evidenced by some of the mail I receive. It is
still supposed by some people that when an addressee is listed
with the title of "Dr.," that "Dr." must of course be a man!
So I am given a wife and the envelope is addressed (by a
computer, I'd like to think!) "Dr. and Mrs. Mary Key."
Some businesses seem to be seeking a more ambiguous way
of directing their communications, and it is not infrequent
now to receive mail addressed "For the Family at...."

There is also an attempt recently to do away with
titles that reflect status, such as "Prof." or "Dr." as well

as marital status.   This puts one in the interesting position
of using or not using the first name.   So some correspondents
are trying the salutation, "Dear Mary Key," a form not heard
of until recently.   In scholarly articles, reference to the work
of male scholars is made by using the last name only.   When
the reference is to a female, there is a difference in practice,
sometimes using the first name also, "Jane Doe" or else a
title "Miss Doe." Seldom is the last name used alone, though
recent publications show a marked change in practice, now
using last name alone for all scholars.   The matter of listing
people has also been a source of different treatment.   In a
recent publication reporting a conference for librarians, the
women participants were listed by title, either Miss or Mrs.,
and the men participants were listed with no title.   Another
practice is to list males with initials and females with first
names.   I was told once, seriously, to use initials instead
of first name in my publications, and it is likely that some
woman scholars follow this practice so that they won't be
known as women.   Later, when we consider the writings of
women, we see that this was prompted by the less enthusiastic response to women as writers and scholars. [52]

In English-speaking countries, most commonly a woman loses her own name with marriage.   On the day of the
wedding she becomes "Mrs." Like the slaves of old, she
takes the name of the man who "owns" her.   This naming
system is not found in all areas.   In Scotland, a woman does
not lose her own name altogether when she marries.   Her
name is written both ways in legal documents. [53] In the
Dutch naming system the woman did not change her name
upon marriage. [54] In Spanish-speaking countries a woman
retains her own name after marriage, adding her husband's
surname after her own.   Therefore when Julia Martinez
marries Juan Gomez, her name is Julia Martinez de Gomez. [55]
When I was in Mexico I heard the amused, giggling reaction
of a young lady who came across the American title, "Mrs.
George Smith." That was the joke of the day--to call a
woman by a man's name!   It does seem ludicrous, come to
think of it, for married women to be known only by men's
names.   Some day we will realize that it is quite absurd
for newspapers to give account of events that take place in
the Women's Club and list those who attend as: Mmes.
Richard Tucker, Lloyd Wright, Pablo Picasso, and Lawrence
Olivier.

The whole business of titles and proper names is a
problem for divorced women, but not for men, who retain

their identity throughout their lifetime.   The legal hassle of
getting back a maiden name is costly.   In addition, if the
woman has established business contacts, or has her silver
engraved, or has professional connections and has published,
it is awkward to continue using a name which no longer belongs to her.   Nowadays when people are living longer and
marrying more often, and if the practice of a woman taking
her husband's name continues, it might be necessary to add
another identifying feature, such as dates, because "Mrs.
John Doe" could be any of several women.   We would have
then, Mrs. John Doe, 1946; Mrs. John Doe, 1953; Mrs.
John Doe, 1963; and Mrs. John Doe, 1971....

     The matter of naming the newborn infant is another
aspect of our naming system which is coming into question
these days.   Rousseau, who believed that his children belonged only to him, would not be very popular today.   For
an infant to take the mother's name would make infinitely
more sense, because that is the only certain relationship by
blood.   Genealogies have been irredeemably altered because
of the patriarchal naming system.   Throughout the ages women have borne infants who were sired by a secret or unknown father.   Historically, this has occurred often among
the upper classes, where divorce was unthinkable but sex
was not.   Thus, often the name which the child carried for
a lifetime was no blood relationship.   If every newborn took
the mother's name, there would be no question.   Anthropologist Margaret Mead has observed that there is a greater
tendency to name the son for the father than to name the
daughter for the mother. [56]   This practice is reinforced because of the complications of having to refer to the mother
as "big" or "old," a situation which is acceptable for males:
"Big John" or "Old John. "

     Another title has swept the country in the last few years,
that is the title "Ms. "   The obligation for females to declare
their marital status by title is of long standing.   In the early
tax records of our country, widows were listed with no personal name of their own: Widow McManemy, Widow Ingman.
The title "Ms. " is a challenge to this practice of women being
listed in relationship to their men.   Actually the title is not
new, though most of us did not realize that it occurred in
secretarial handbooks decades ago.   A national TV newscaster
further noted that it was used by "junk mail" advertisers !
This kind of association by juxtaposition has a powerful affect
on the thinking of the listeners and how they are to accept this
title and the human beings represented by the title.

The reactions to the title "Ms." have run the full
range of human emotions, from wide, joyful acceptance, to
outrageous rejection. Nevertheless it has found its way into
the dictionary. Delicious jokes and marvelous advertising
have resulted from Ms. One company sells a little carry-all
bag as a "Ms. Kit." A newspaper headlined the "Ms.-Match"
of Billie Jean King and Bobby Riggs. The title "Ms." has
proliferated very fast in professional circles and among young
women. Married men are said not to like it. [57] Nevertheless,
it is being used on official documents and forms published by
prestigious businesses and government. A plural form has
been generated: "Mses." Analogous forms in other languages
have started. In Denmark, the form is "Fr.," which is an
abbreviation of both "Fru" (Mrs.) and "Frøken" (Miss). In
France the equivalent is "Mad." In Spanish-speaking countries
the form is "Sa.", the abbreviation of "Sra." (Mrs.) and
"Srta." (Miss).

The pronunciation of the title "Ms." accommodates very
well to the phonological system of the English language, where
fast-speech forms are commonly found in natural speech, and
sounds are neutralized or less distinct. The result is a tele-
scoped "Mizz", using only one syllable as in "Miss" and using
the same final z sound of "Mrs." This rhymes with other
words commonly used in English, such as "his" (hiz) and
"whizz." Actually the pronunciation "Miz" (and other variants)
is already in use for the title "Mrs." in some parts of the
South and occasionally in New England. [58] It occurs in the
speech of cultivated, educated people throughout these areas.
The geographical differences of pronunciation are similar to
the geographical distribution of /greasy/ and /greazy/. The
neutralized pronunciation has the effect of obliterating the contrastive titles "Mrs." and "Miss" and the result is a single
pronunciation for both. One could say that the South is ahead
of the nation in this respect! A further observation, made
some years ago, is that the "z" pronunciation was gaining
usage. It will be interesting to follow the development of
the pronunciation of these titles now that the "Ms." form
is being introduced across the nation. The pronunciation of
"Ms." has received unkind attacks by some who hear it as
a very ugly combination. Interestingly enough these judgments
have not been made on the way Southerners or New Englanders
pronounce "Miss" or "Mrs."

Objections made about the pronunciation of Ms., or
the outrage of the insecure married man or woman who needs
the married title for his or her security blanket are really

trivial matters in comparison with the underlying problems
brought to the surface by the attention given to the title "Ms."
Even if Ms. were widely accepted throughout all of society,
the real problem of sex differentiation and discrimination is
still there.   And this is where the real trouble lies.   There
have been several suggestions lately that we do away with
titles altogether.   I think this might be the most unrealistic
suggestion--with the givens of human nature.   Titles, like
all symbols, are important because they are a reminder of
what they represent.   Besides designating the human condition,
titles are useful symbols to establish credentials.   We know
a person has certain qualifications with respect to occupational demands by means of a title.   A person with an M. D.
is qualified to treat illness, and this is extremely useful information.   In fact, a good case could be made for needing
more titles in a burgeoning society.   Long ago, in the villages,
one knew who was qualified to shoe the horses, because one
grew up with this information.   Today it is a gamble to find
a competent person to tune the piano, to teach dancing lessons,
to sell the right size shoe, or to fix the TV.   Titles that
imply a certain training and expertise would be helpful.

        Hardly anyone would disagree with the use of titles
for this kind of information.   The confusion and disagreement
comes in the area of status and having to declare the state
of the human being: sex and marital condition.   With regard
to status, all languages of the world have some way of indicating status among human beings.   This is done by use of
titles, proper names, honorifics on nouns, pronoun use, and
many other linguistic forms.   This must be mentioned here
in this study because of the inextricable relationship of sex
distinctions and status values.   Many people do not like status
distinctions, but they are universal--so far no human society
has found a way to do away with them.   Some have tried.
After World War II the Russians tried to do away with titles
among the Hungarians, but apparently have given up recently.
A language textbook published in 1965 gives the titles "com-
rade" and "colleague" and then goes on to say, "The courtesy
title úr Mr. or Sir fell into disuse after 1947, but today it
is slowly coming back into the language."[59] Perhaps status,
like sex, is an inevitable category which we must learn to
cope with rather than do away with.

        The title "Mrs." and the wedding ring are symbols
of the human condition--reminders that there is a commitment.
The title "Ms." has focused attention on the glaring discrepancy that males are not required to wear a symbol of

commitment--either the wedding ring or a title, since "Mr."
does not reflect marital status. A suggestion has been made
that would balance this disequilibrium to some extent: that
another title be devised which would indicate whether or not
men are married. I think by far, this is the most desirable
suggestion and very practical, though I don't see men rushing
out to find and adopt such a title! It would be delightfully
helpful to women, however--they would know who to spend
their time with at conventions and on vacation trips.   This
suggestion is not new either.   In 1941 the journal American
Speech published some remarks on the topic following the
account of a newspaper which defended the title "Mk." which
stood for "Mark", which means "a mark worth shooting at."
The journal seriously suggested "Br." or "Bch." for "bachelor."

     Still earlier, a satirist of the turn of the century de-
fined titles in a work he was collecting called The Devil's
Dictionary.[60]   These bits and pieces were published in newspapers and recently compiled in a complete work.   Under
the entry for "Miss" he offers:

> A title with which we brand unmarried women to
> indicate that they are in the market.   Miss, Missis
> (Mrs.) and Mister (Mr.) are the three most dis-
> tinctly disagreeable words in the language in sound
> and sense.   Two are corruptions of Mistress, the
> other of Master.   In the general abolition of social
> titles in this our country they miraculously escaped
> to plague us.   If we must have them let us be con-
> sistent and give one to the unmarried man.   I
> venture to suggest Mush, abbreviated to Mh.

     Whatever the final outcome is, let us hope that it
will be something that will avoid situations such as the following.   Before the title Ms. became familiar a conversation
with an airline office took place where the clerk insisted on
putting a title before the name of the person buying the tick-
et.   The woman buyer in turn insisted that she did not want
to be titled either "Miss" or "Mrs."   Thereby the clerk
said, "Well, then, I'll have to put "Mr."   In another conversation on the radio the other day I heard an interviewer
talking to a woman on the telephone.   He said, "I don't
know if you're "Miss" or "Mrs., so I'll call you Karen."

     In the meantime, ingenious, creative females are
going to find ways to cope.   An enterprising young woman

on Wall Street found one solution. [61]   When she phones to
talk with an important head of a company, secretaries, of
course, ask who is calling.   She simply says, "Tell him its
MiMi."   Without delay she gets through to the executive.
"It would never work," she explains, "if I said, 'Miss
Green'."

Chapter VI

DISCRIMINATION AGAINST MALES, TABOOS, AND THE DOUBLE STANDARD

What are little boys made of?
Snakes and snails, and puppy-dogs' tails;
And that's what little boys are made of.

Attention has been drawn lately to language facts which show that females are discriminated against. It is not difficult to reel off example after example of malicious terms that refer only to females and their lot in life as sex objects. Careful observation, however, will show that males also suffer discrimination in subtle and devastating ways. The verbal environment can be hostile to them. In one of my university classes not long ago, we discussed the honor system and the matter of how to deal with cheating. Several minutes of frank, open discussion went on with illustrations and hypothetical situations honestly discussed. At the end of the discussion, it occurred to us that whenever a "cheater" had been referred to, the pronoun referent was "he" and whenever a non-cheater had been referred to, the pronoun referent was "she." The on-a-pedestal image of women still controls the thinking of this generation! The female is the sinless, untouchable, model of purity, dressed in white and uplifted out of reach. Conversely, the male is the sinful, vulgar model of deceit.

Shortly after that incident I heard a newscaster refer to the "enemy" as "he": "The enemy has the capability to launch attacks if he chooses to do so...." Other language expressions come to mind that have been repeated through the generations: "Boys don't cry!" "Boys will be boys!" "No real man would do that!" There is a long list of nouns which embody a male referent: bad boy, bastard, bully, bum, cad, coward, criminal, dare devil, gambler, goblin, good-for-nothing, Peeping Tom, rascal, rogue, sissy, sneak thief, thief, tramp, villain. There is a long list of insulting terms which are highly offensive to males, such as "shmuck,"

THE ALUMNAE

"It's what is known as a girl-cott."

By Mary Gauerke; copyright © 1972 by The Register and
Tribune Syndicate; reproduced by permission.

---

borrowed from the Yiddish language.

If a male uses tender, expressive, gentle language,
he is ridiculed and laughed right out of the locker-room.
That males should be associated with negative and unpleasant
concepts and females with goodness and purity is unreality
at its best.   And of course, such an unreal model breaks
down with glaring paradoxes as we compare illustrations such
as these with the quotation from Pythagoras at the beginning
of the book: "good principle = man; evil principle = woman."
No wonder, then, that mankind is schizophrenic and irrational
about male and female concepts.   Perhaps the most remarkable thing about the situation we are in is that it has gone
on as long as it has with acceptance.   One wonders why
human beings--male and female--haven't challenged these limiting value judgments long ago.

The taboos of a society revolve around fears and conflicts that the society has difficulties in coping with.   This
includes such things as sex, death, age, power, money, race,
certain gods, certain relationships, and failure of a space
missile.   The connection between female language and taboos

is unquestionable, [62] though it should be remembered that some
taboos restrict the language of males also.   Restraints, prohibitions, and forbidden vocabulary items apparently are found
in every language of the world.   Men's use of taboo expressions
among themselves may be restricted in the presence of women and children.   In our own culture, taboos involve most
acutely the matters of sex, body elimination, and body parts.
The prohibited domains are not necessarily the same in other
cultures or subcultures.   Among the mountain people of the
Ozarks the names of male animals: bull, boar, buck, ram,
jack, stallion, are never spoken in the presence of women. [63]
Among the Mayo people of northern Mexico, women are not
supposed to know many of the words connected with certain
rituals. [64]   Taboo restrictions and control measures have a
close relationship in social structures.   The Mundurucú of
South America have a strongly male-oriented culture.   The
sacred musical instruments which are used in secret rituals,
and are taboo to the sight of the women, have "significance
in the rationalization of sex roles and the validation of the
superordinate position of the male. "[65]

        Unreal and cruel dichotomizing in language behavior
inevitably leads to double standards in the treatment of male
and female in every aspect of language use.   Previously we
noted the difference in use of labels and titles and names
(Chapter V).   This difference also illustrates a double standard.   One often hears on the news that women are referred
to by their first names.   We all heard about the activities
of "Betty" and "Bess" when referring to the work of Betty
Furness and Bess Myerson.   But we never hear about "Bobby, John, and Melvin" when the news report concerns Messrs.
Finch, Connally, and Laird.

        Job titles and classifications are different depending
upon whether male or female fills the position.   A male is
an "assistant manager"; a female is an "administrative assistant. " A female professor will be "Mrs. Doe" while her
husband (on the same campus!) is "Prof. Doe. "   Descriptions of male and female have a different ring to them: an
older woman has "wrinkles" but an older man has "deep
crevices. " Euphemisms are created out of the restrictions
of taboos. The matter of handling taboo words is changing
fast though. Dictionaries used to print tabooed sexual and
body elimination words with dashes or asterisks represent-
ing some letters--leaving enough hints to recognize the
forms. The last decade has seen significant changes in
the written and spoken use of these forms.   The double

standard still exists, however.   Just within the last two years
I was advised not to use the word "Damn" in a linguistic illustration, because it made me sound like a feminist!   Linguists
and innovators who will not permit the Procrustean bed to be
imposed on the language variety of other segments of the population sometimes have difficulty not continuing to hold women
in an analogous Procrustean cradle.   Female comedians, too,
feel a double-standard response to their desire to use the full
range of language.   Their material is restricted as a result
and intimidation continues to haunt those who advocate change
in language standards.

     The matter of description of people and the interpreta-
tion of human qualities is based for instance on this double
standard.   A bold man is courageous but a bold woman is
aggressive.   A student pointed out to me that one can say of
a woman who is easy to seduce, "She's easy" but one cannot
say "He's easy. "   A person who is innovative is "pushy" if
female, but "original" if male.   If insistent, a female is hysterical, but a male is persistent.   If politically involved, a
female is over-emotional, a male is committed. [66]

     Again, the double standard and the Madonna/Whore
syndrome prevail in the use of really expressive and angry
language ("swear words" and "four-letter words").   Women
are permitted only such daring expressions as "Oh shoot, "
"Oh fudge, " "Heck, " and "Golly. "   Men are given free
reign--but not in front of women and children.   It is a
gallant but untenable notion that women should be "protected"
from rough language.   The vocabulary denied the female
has to do with functions she is very much familiar with.
One wonders what on earth she is being protected from,
when, at the same time she is at the center of action,
cleaning up the blood, vomit, and refuse, as she nurtures
others through birth, sickness, and death.   On the other
hand, she is denied full language expression to vent her own
emotions.   Women must not get angry enough to swear!   Could
it be that this kind of prescriptive restriction results in the
depressive behavior so common among females?

     The illogicality of roles permitted male and female
shows up in language.   A male is supposed to be "protective"
and a real man wouldn't think of permitting a woman to support him.   A female is supposed to be the one who "nurtures. "   Note that the semantic components underlying
these words are very much the same.   But the words differ
in use.   The linguistic form "protecting" is more likely to

be used in taking care of countries or borders. It is quite possible that the desire to take care of is a human trait which is found in all people at the same time that an opposing trait of wanting to be taken care of is also found in all human beings.

All human beings, then, are in great need of being liberated from a linguistic confinement contrary to human nature. As males become more aware of the discriminations against them, they will begin to appreciate the changes taking place. I can think of no better way to conclude this section than to quote a fine, sensitive young man who asked me, "How would you feel if you were taught that you were made of snails and puppy-dog tails"?

Chapter VII

EARLY EDUCATION AND LANGUAGE ABILITY

At some point in our discussion of male/female differences we have to ask, When does it all begin? Even before a baby is born, it begins to respond to stimuli from
the world which it does not yet know. [67] Carefully conducted
experiments have shown that movement of a fetus increases
in response to sounds made near the abdomen of the mother.
This response is clearly established by the eighth month and
increases as the time for birth approaches. After birth the
infant verily thrives on human contact; indeed the interrela-
tionship between infant and other humans seems to be as
necessary as food itself for growth and maturing. There is
some evidence that language progress is impeded without
the warm communication of care-taker to infant. [68] The care-
taker, of course, is the mother in most instances, but other
human surrogates can substitute in this communicative relationship. In fact, a warm communicative substitute would
be preferable to a cold, noncommunicative mother. It is
a commonplace among observers of infant behavior that social
behavior and response are well established before the infant
is a year old.

At what age does imitative behavior, which leads to
language learning, begin? Undoubtedly the fact that there
are individual differences has resulted in the various ages
cited by investigators. One well-documented case described
imitative behavior in a nine-week-old infant. [69] Many hints
throughout the literature point to an even earlier age. In
my own experiences with new-born babes, I have observed
responsive behavior much earlier, but exactly when this
responsive behavior also becomes imitative is still an open
question. The personalities of the new-born and the care-
taker are involved. The amount of time that the care-taker
has to stimulate and respond to the baby is involved. If
there are other children to care for, and if household duties
are very demanding, the care-taker, or mother, may not
actually have much time for the "practice sessions" which

"Congratulations! It's a beautiful human being."

By Michael Heath; copyright © 1973 by Punch Magazine;
reproduced by permission of the Los Angeles Times Syndicate.

---

elicit vocal response.   Other children in the surroundings
and the interest, or absence, of the father, and others, all
contribute to the development of the infant's response to the
external world.   There are several ways in which a neonate
learns to respond to other humans in the course of developing communication systems.   First of all, rhythm is established very early, perhaps before birth.   A study of biological rhythms speaks of "fetal activity rhythms" and further
states that time sense and rhythm develop before language. [70]
Wolff, a well-known researcher in infant behavior, has established the stability of rhythm in infant cries during the neo-
natal period. [71]   Since rhythm is an important component of
language, and differs from language to language, we must
assume the importance of vocalizations in this stage of the
development of the infant.

Pitch differences also occur in the vocal response of

the infant very early.   These, with various mixes of rhythm,
form the basis of intonation patterns later in speech.   The
intonation features of language are like the melody of a lilting
song, complete with rhythm and emphasis.   Infant observers
have noted pitch response from two months on.   A linguist
at Stanford University studied recordings of the babblings and
gurglings of Chinese, Russian, and American babies. [72]   At
a half-year old, the Chinese babies were producing vocalizations significantly different from those of the babies reared
in the other language environments.   The utterances of the
Chinese babies were usually of the single syllable type with
vowel-like sounds dominating and with a great deal of pitch
variation over a single "syllable" or vowel sound.   This type
of pitch variation is typical of the Chinese language.   In contrast, the babies in Russian- and English-speaking environments showed little pitch variation over single syllables--
typical of the Russian and English languages.

Facial expressions also figure in the communicative
response of infants at a very early age.   It is not clear
whether infants respond sooner, and better, to visual or to
auditory stimuli.   Probably some infants respond slightly better to visual, as do some adults; and some infants respond
better to auditory, as do some adults.   Or perhaps they vary
according to time of day, fatigue, amount of light--i.e., aspects of the context of situation.   Movement and touch also
figure in the communicative aspects of infant and other human
interaction.   None of these channels of communicating occurs
alone or exclusively.   Before an infant learns language, he
or she is learning social differences in expression and response to other humans--that is, the infant not only responds
to humans but makes different responses to different categories of persons, depending upon the sex and relationship.
The various channels of communication mentioned above are
manipulated in various ways to produce different responses.

Very few studies have been done with regard to sex
differences, but from the evidence available, it is obvious
that learned sex differences begin very early in life.   More
research needs to be done to understand at what age the infant learned them, how these differences are conveyed to the
infant, and to what extent, and how important they are to the
development of the child.   Lieberman tells of one such study
that is significant. [73]   Using the sound spectrograph, the
fundamental frequencies, which indicate pitch differences, were
measured on the babblings of two infants.   Recordings were
made of a ten-month-old boy and a thirteen-month-old girl

under several different conditions. Of interest to us here
are the recordings made while "talking" to the mother and
to the father. The babies' fathers used lower average fundamental frequencies, or lower pitch, than their mothers.
In imitation the babies responded with lower pitch to the fathers and higher pitch to the mothers.

Other important studies have been done recently[74]
that indicate very definite differences in adult behavior toward
male and female infants. The pink and blue blanket are applied from birth on. For example, mothers touch boy babies
more than they touch girls. An interpretation of this fact
is difficult to make. A biased opinion would be a simple
answer: male infants are more valuable. This is too easy.
It does not explain why male infants also cry more and are
more fretful. Nor does it explain why males are comforted
more by touch while female infants may be comforted by
voice alone. As the infants develop, differential treatment
continues; this perhaps reinforces any physiological differences
which the babies started out with. One-year-old girls stay
closer to mother with more touching behavior than their one-
year-old brothers.

Studies done on the phonetic development of sounds by
infants in the process of language learning do not show a significant difference in the ability and development of male and
female infants.[75] Some studies show slight differences, with
sometimes the girls exceeding the boys, and other studies
show the boys exceeding the girls. None of the differences
is statistically significant, and with the almost infinite range
of given variables possible in the experimental set ups, it
has never been established that there is any universal sex
difference in performance in gaining control of the sounds
of a language.

With regard to words and the building up of words,
the same conclusions are drawn.[76] Berko studied the language performance of children according to certain morphological rules.[77] She made up nonsense "words" and then
elicited responses from the children which would indicate their
ability to expand the words to make up such linguistic constructions as plurals, past tense, progressive forms, and
possessives. For example, to elicit the plural form, she
showed the child a picture of a make-believe character, saying, "This is a wug." Then she showed the child a picture
with two of these characters, and encouraged the child to
finish the sentence, "Now there are two _____."

The child added the plural morpheme "wugs," as was expected. Similarly she elicited verbal forms by showing pictures
and saying, "This is a man who knows how to zib. What is
he doing? He is _____. " In the final analysis, with
all things considered, it turned out that the boy and girl performance was practically equal.

    As far as speech styles are concerned, there are ob-
servable differences between boys and girls at a very early
age. This can be seen, for example, when youngsters play
house, or play store, and they modify their own speech by
code switching according to the role they are playing. Again,
there is concrete evidence that adults talk differently to male
and female children. In an important study done at Harvard,[78]
tape recordings were made in the homes of five families with
several children, to observe speech styles of the very young.
The conclusions were that:

> Fathers and mothers did not talk in exactly the
> same way to the babies, and there seemed to be
> some sex differences as well in how the babies
> were addressed. Some of the boy babies were
> addressed, especially by their fathers, in a sort
> of Hail-Baby-Well-Met style: while turning them
> upside down or engaged in similar play, the fathers
> said things like 'Come here, you little nut!' or 'Hey
> fruitcake!' Baby girls were dealt with more gently,
> both physically and verbally.

    From the pre-language stages, then, and during early
language acquisition, boys and girls advance in language development at generally the same rate; the differences can be
attributed to individual performance rather than to sex. Nevertheless, during these periods, the children have plenty of
opportunity to establish well-defined sex differences in language as well as other behavior. Nursery rhymes and fairy
tales reinforce the differences; toys, colors of clothes, and
play equipment establish the behavior differences beyond a
shadow of a doubt.

    By the time children enter school, the sex patterns
are very well entrenched. School activities in every dimension continue to emphasize the male-female dichotomy. An
alphabet-teaching program, for example, was recently introduced to the schools as a bright new way to learn letters.
The inflatable, plastic figures represented personalities: the
vowels are female characters and the consonants are all males.

School-related activities reinforce the separation of the sexes.
In 1971, at one elementary school in Los Angeles, no less
than twelve organizations which are sex-segregated distributed
invitations to the children on the school premises. [79]

These cultural differences of sex role and expectations
make an effect on the performance of boys and girls during
the early school years and continue to mark performance
throughout the teens. Studies invariably show that in language
skills girls do better than boys in the early years of schooling.
Boys constitute 75 to 85 per cent of the youngsters who have
reading problems or who are in remedial classes. More
boys stutter than girls. [80] Educational scholars have observed
that although children of the same age vary widely in language
proficiency, some factors produce differences. Dawson and
Newman report that "Retardation in language growth ... may
be due to (1) having unusually low intelligence, (2) being shy
... (3) being a twin or triplet ... (4) being a boy ... (5)
coming from a home in which experiences are barren...." [81]
Maccoby further elaborates in her study of sex differences in
intellectual functioning and verbal ability:

> Through the preschool years and in the early school
> years, girls exceed boys in most aspects of verbal
> performance. They say their first word sooner,
> articulate more clearly and at an earlier age, use
> longer sentences, and are more fluent. By the be-
> ginning of school, however, there are no longer any
> consistent differences in vocabulary. Girls learn
> to read sooner, and there are more boys than girls
> who require special training in remedial reading
> programs; but by approximately the age of ten, a
> number of studies show that boys have caught up
> in their reading skills. Throughout the school
> years, girls do better on tests of grammar, spelling,
> and word fluency. [82]

One explanation for the boy/girl performance is offered
by Sexton, who believes that the schools are too feminized:

> School words tend to be the words of women. They
> have their own sound and smell, perfumed or anti-
> septic. Boys usually prefer touch and colorful short
> words--while teachers and girls lean toward longer,
> more floral, opaque synonyms. School words are
> clean, refined, idealized and as remote from phys-
> ical things as the typical schoolmarm from the tough

> realities of ordinary life.
>   Active words usage, as in <u>speaking,</u> is usually
> discouraged in school; students are expected to
> speak only when addressed. Even boys who refuse
> to read or write usually like to talk, but on their
> own terms. It is the school's most troublesome
> job to keep boys quiet and in their seats. [83]

Hall offers the suggestion that some grammatical rules
came to be linked with sex distinctions; men and boys said
"can" and women and girls said "may." "'May' naturally
sounded more refined to the women so they insisted on foisting
it on the men along with a lot of gobbledygook about possible
and not possible."[84] Whatever the immediate explanation, it
lies in the pattern of cultural factors regarding expectations
and roles of male and female. In cultures where the education of girls is not important, the results are different, and
boys excell in language skills. Stanchfield points this out in
her extensive study of the sexual factor in language development and reading: "Further support for cultural explanation
of these differences has been reported by Paul S. Anderson
who observed that in Japan, where male children are given
preferential attention in both home and school, the language
development of boys is more advanced than that of girls."[85]

At the other end of the school spectrum girls have to
decide when, if, and how much of their skills to depress.
When the desire for "femininity" and appeal to the male sex
dominates their thinking, they begin to underplay their capac-
ities and attainments, and indeed, even fail to attain. In
general, "with an increase in age the boys have a progressively poorer relative opinion of the girls and the girls have
a progressively better relative opinion of the boys."[86] Shortly
after World War II cultural contradictions and sex roles were
studied among college women. Large numbers of the coeds
were found to have

>   ... 'played dumb' on dates, that is, concealed some
> academic honor, pretended ignorance of some sub-
> ject, or allowed the man the last word in an intel-
> lectual discussion. Among these were women who
> 'threw games' and in general played down certain
> skills in obedience to the unwritten law that men
> must possess these skills to a superior degree. [87]

The situation doesn't seem to have changed much since
then. No wonder, when the stereotypes of society are foisted
upon them daily. The following is a quotation from a college

textbook used in classes on writing and style: "Underlining
is generally described as 'feminine,' by which it is to be
inferred that no real man would make use of it for fear of
being thought womanly, while no real woman would use it
either, because it is unmanly."[88]

    In an excellent review of child development research,
a well-known scholar surveyed the studies done on sex role
identification and intellectual mastery.[89] He noted, for example, that the degree of academic involvement is greater
for adolescent and adult males than for females. It is well
documented that skills such as spatial and mechanical rea-
soning, science, and mathematics are considered more appropriate for boys than for girls. Many studies show that girls
perform less well in these areas. The obvious connection
with cultural conditioning was exemplified by studies which
showed that the females who rejected traditional feminine
interests performed better on mathematical and geometric
problems, in contradistinction to the typical female, whose
motivation to attack such problems is low. The researcher
concluded that the construct of sex role identification is not
without its ambiguity, but that "Its retention as a descriptive
and explanatory concept rests on the assumption that the
concepts male and female and the dimensions maleness and
femaleness are basic to our language." Apparently there is
a basic desire for congruence between an ideal representa-
tion of the self and one's everyday behavior. Also there
appears to be a basic need for cognitive harmony and balance.
Thus, one learns in unconscious imitation to follow patterns
of long standing, even though the results may lead to enormous
contradictions and doublebinds which are unbearable. Education, then, will have to deal with changes to sex role standards that will be more compatible with the actualities of
human beings.

    Before we leave the matter of sex differences in ed-
ucation, let us consider the global problem of illiteracy--
"Woman's Worldwide Burden." It is a well-known fact that
it is difficult to interpret the figures on literacy, in that
the measures are different from country to country. Some
figures for literacy are given on the basis of the ability to
write one's name, while other tests for literacy demand that
the person be able to read a paragraph from the newspaper.
Thus, the figures betray us. But it is not unreasonable to
say that about half of the population of the world cannot read
materials such as simple readers, pamphlets on birth control,
or health brochures, much less articles of laws and legis-

lation that protect the vulnerable.

Of this half of the world's population who cannot read, most of the persons involved are females.   The figures vary from country to country, with nearly 100 per cent female illiteracy in some underdeveloped countries to about a parity in countries such as ours.   An editorial from Saturday Review paints a gloomy picture: "In a tragic sense, the vast majority of the women of the world are doomed, even today, because of their sex and because they are separated from the rudiments of their own written language. "[90]

Chapter VIII

SUBJECTS, NOT OBJECTS:
LINGUISTIC STRUCTURES[91]

Up until now we have talked mostly about language as
it functions in the inter-relationships between human beings
who use language patterns that are fairly obvious, even to
the casual observer. These surface structures result from
the mind and thought, from basic attitudes and belief systems
which are, for the most part, out-of-awareness. The question we now ask is whether or not male and female differences
also occur in linguistic structures of language, or do they
only occur in stylistic structures, variations in expressions,
and choice of vocabulary? Do these differences occur in the
form of language as well as the function?

Linguistic structures generally are investigated along
the lines of the three basic components of language: phonological (or pronunciation) features, grammatical features, and
semantic (or meaning) features. The first two of these kinds
of features are more easily analyzed and are dealt with rather handily as the data are more obvious. The semantic features, however, involve underlying conceptual categories that
give meaning to linguistic performance. These features, in
any language, are far more difficult to understand; scientists,
in fact, are not yet able to do machine translation, except
in the rawest stages, because of these complex semantic
structures which have not been completely analyzed in any
language.

Phonological

The phonological component includes, roughly, that
which is involved in pronunciation, the articulation of sounds,
as it were. In some languages, in some words, males and
females pronounce some sounds with distinct patterns. [92]
Among speakers of Cham in Vietnam, in women's speech,
/r/ becomes /y/ in some circumstances, for example, in
initial consonant clusters; /b/ and /d/ are preglottalized;

initial /y/ may be glottalized.

In the Gros Ventre language of Montana (see below) it was reported certain affricate sounds, such as /tc, dj (ty)/, in the speech of men were pronounced as velars /k and ky/ in the speech of women. Pronunciation changes involve pitch differences as well as change of consonant in Koasati, a Muskogean language of southwestern Louisiana (next page).

Sapir gives several examples of differences of pronunciation in the Yana Indian Language of California (see next page).

"Busy career wives take us house-husbands for granted! . . . We need affection and understanding as well as being sex objects!"

By George Lichty; copyright © 1973 by Field Enterprises, Inc.; reproduced courtesy of Publishers-Hall Syndicate.

	Cham Men	Cham Women
day	hray	hyay
new	praw	pyaw
ring	korah	koyah
to scratch	koraw	koyaw

	Gros Ventre Men	Gros Ventre Women
newborn child	wadjínsihiθa	wakínsihiθa
Upper Quarters (name of band)	idjiθan	ikiθan
his gum	itcénibitc	ikénibik
abundant grass	djáaθa	kyáaθa
bread	dja'tsa	kya'tsa
stones	ʌʌnædjæn	ʌʌnǽkyæn
someone's pinto horse	tcætcʌniθibiætc	kyækyʌniθibiæk

	Koasati Men	Koasati Women
"I am lifting it"	lakawwís	lakawwíl
"we are peeling it"	molhís	molhíl
"lift it !" (said to 2nd person pl.)	lakawhós	lakawhôl

Yana Male	Yana Female

mô'i "to eat"   môt^i

imamba "deer liver"   imampt^a

wawip!a "little house"   wawip!a

sigāga "quail"   sigākt^a

gāgi "crow"   gākt^i

mal'gu "ear"   mal'kt^u

p'adja "snow"   p'atct^a

mits!i "coyote"   mits!t^l

dāha "river"   daxt^a

'īsi "man"   'ist^l

cūcu "dog, horse"   cūct^u

ts!orêwa "elk"   ts!orêwt^a

'iya "trail"   'iyt^a

wêyu "horn"   we yt^u

'ī'lala "star"   'i'lalt^a

īwulu "inside"   iwult^u

wak!ara "moon"   wak!art^a

p'att!ama "bird sp. "   p'att!amt^a

ba'nīnu "dentalia"   ba'nint^u

'ak!āli'li "lake"   'ak!ālilt^i

mari'mi "woman"   mari'm

Differences of pronunciation also occur in languages of India. The sounds of Bengali have been recorded and it is noted that "In the speech of women and children and of the uneducated classes there is a tendency ... to pronounce an 'n' for an 'l', in initial positions. "[93]

In English, differences are perhaps more subtle, but they also occur. The pronunciation of the ending "-ing, " for example, is articulated differently at times, by male and female. In a study done with children, the "-ing" pronunciation symbolized female speakers, and the "-in" pronunciation symbolized male speakers. The variations between the pronunciations, however, were not solely sex-differentiated, but were intricately involved with status, personality,

mood, formality, and specific verbs. Verbs associated with
the "-ing" pronunciation were: criticizing, correcting, reading, visiting, interesting. Verbs associated with the "-in"
pronunciation were: punchin, flubbin, swimmin, chewin, hit-
tin. [94] The semantic categories are obvious; one can further
extrapolate on the interest domains permitted boys and girls!

A study of speech in Detroit was concerned with the
fronting of the three vowels, /æ, a, ɔ/, among various
socio-economic classes, [95] and it was found that women out-
scored the men in fronting these vowels--another example of
status intersecting with sex dimensions. Significant male/
female differences also showed up in the pronunciation or
absence of /r/ in various studies. [96] A surprising conclusion was that changes of pronunciation were initiated by young
women, a fact which fosters speculation regarding language
change.

A feature of pronunciation is the pattern of supraseg-
mentals or intonation, elements of pitch, length, and stress,
found in all languages of the world. No linguistic study has
ever indicated basic differences in male/female intonation
patterns in English, which are exclusively one or the other,
as, for example, one might find in vocabulary differences.
The differences are quantitative; that is, there are prefer-
ences and avoidances of particular patterns. It would not be
surprising to find individual patterns that would correspond
to other idiolectal features already observed in other levels
of language expressions. Students of languages recognize
that there are individual characteristics and predilections for
certain grammatical constructions and typical vocabulary use.
Some persons, for example, use a great many hesitation patterns or uncertainty patterns. Some individuals use a high
percentage of patterns that communicate such traits as coyness, bull-headedness, cheerfulness, and sarcasm. It is
likely that these linguistic features correlate with personality
types. It is also quite likely that women use patterns of uncertainty and indefiniteness more often than men--patterns of
plight. That this is so is indicated by phoneticians who suggest that the "raised, weak syllables" are said to be a "woman's intonation. "[97]

Of the several patterns of intonation that dominate in
women's speech, it will be noted that many or most of them
fall into the areas of emotional, expressive language. Thus,
the learned intonational features make women appear to be
more emotional. Contrasts with the emotional language of

men will be seen later as we discuss pronoun references.
Another feature of the intonation of women's speech is a tendency to speak in an overall high pitch on the part of some
women. In many cases, the pitch of women and children are
comparable. In addition, within a range of the person's norm,
women used the highest level of pitch (the excited pitch) more
than men. That women do speak with more expressive intonational patterns has been noted by some pilot studies and ob-
server-linguists. In a brief exploratory experiment a student
of mine listened to children in the third, fourth, and fifth
grades retell a story. The girls spoke with very expressive
intonation, and the boys toned down the intonational features,
even to the point of monotony, "playing it cool." A study of
adult intonation patterns [98] corroborates this differentiation.
Females more often use patterns of surprise, unexpectedness,
cheerfulness, and politeness. The following examples, taken
from this study, often occur in the speech of women:

The unexpectedness and surprise pattern:

'O\h 'tha\t's 'aw\ful!

A non-final pattern:

I know he has| 'g\on/e.

He's coming 'wh/en?

The hesitation pattern:

Well, I/'stu\died...

The polite, cheerful pattern:

Are you 'com/ing?

     Radio and T.V. broadcasting is a career that is con-
cerned with delivery of speech, particularly the features of
pronunciation. Speakers are taught to control the pitch and
quality of the voice in order to sound neutral. A handbook
for announcers [99] states that while women were hired by
radio stations during World War II, they were not retained
after the war because "often the higher-pitched female voices
could not hold listeners' attention for any length of time,
while the lower-pitched voices were frequently vehicles for
an overly polished, ultrasophisticated delivery that sounded
phoney." The handbook goes on to say that "Women's delivery
... is lacking in the authority needed for a convincing newscast...." In Germany and in the South, they have not read
that handbook, though, because women's voices are heard
frequently on the air in both of those areas.

Grammatical

Matters of a grammatical nature have to do with the analysis of how words are constructed--this level of linguistics is called morphology (i. e. , the shape of words). Syntax is the matter of stringing these words together in an orderly arrangement. Male/female differences in morphological patterns have been demonstrated in several languages of the world. Kūrux, a Dravidian language of north India, has such features. The differences in the verb paradigms are based on four possible speech contexts, depending on who speaks to whom: (1) man speaks to man (MM), (2) man speaks to woman (MW), (3) woman speaks to woman (WW), (4) woman speaks to man (WM). The following illustrations show the conjugation of the verb bar- ("come") and show singular and plural persons:[100]

Verb bar-.   Present paradigm

MM	MW	WW	WM
bar-d-an	bar-d-an	bar?-e-n	bar-d-an
bar-d-am	bar-d-am	bar?-e-m	bar-d-am
bar-d-at	bar-d-at	bar-d-at	bar-d-at
bar-d-ay	bar-d-i	bar-d-in	bar-d-ay
bar-d-ar	bar-d-ar	bar-d-ay	bar-d-ar
bar-d-as	bar-d-as	bar-d-as	bar-d-as
bar?-∅-i(d)	bar?-∅-i(d)	bar?-∅-i(d)	bar?-∅-i(d)
bar-n-ar	bar-n-ar	bar-n-ay	bar-n-ar

Cocama, a Tupi language of the Amazon, has a different pronoun series for male and female speakers.[101]

	male	female
this	iquiá	ajan
that	yucá	yucun
I, to me	ta	etse
you, to you	ene	ene
he, she, to him, her	uri	ai
we (incl)	ini	ini
we (excl)	tana	penu
you (pl.), to you	epe	epe
them, to them	rana	inu

English does not have such well-defined differences in

the morphological structures. Nevertheless, there is one
suffix which gives considerable trouble, the ending -ess
to designate the female counterpart of a male "unmarked"
word: poet:poetess, author:authoress. A scholar of the
English language early in this century wrote about "doctress,
authoress, preacheress, astronomess" and other forms which
designate the femaleness of the professional person. She
noted that this problem is of fairly recent origin, in terms
of the long history of the language:

> As soon as woman got out of her rightful place as
> mistress of a home she began to make trouble for
> the writers and speakers who had to mention her
> unwonted doings. What to call a woman who usurp-
> ed man's place in the pulpit, in the practice of
> medicine, in the editing of periodicals, in the writ-
> ing of books, in the jury box, and on the field of
> battle, was a problem for the mid-nineteenth cen-
> tury American writer and speaker. [102]

This confusion in the use of labels led to derogatory
concepts and the "ultra-chivalrous American gentleman ...
stigmatized women workers, wherever he could, with the
suffix -ess. A former president of the Linguistic Society
of America also noted this unpleasant flavor: "To refer to
a woman aviator as an aviatrix sounds quaint nowadays, and
even actress is sometimes dropped in favor of actor--mention
of sex seems inappropriate except for humor or insult."[103]
Another English scholar has discussed the use of the term as
applied to Emily Dickinson and noted, "In the mid-nineteenth
century the term 'poetess' expressed the general feeling that
female nature lacked qualities essential to the creation of
great poetry."[104] This use of the suffix -ess, then, would
automatically exclude female writers of poetry from an an-
thology or collection of "Great Poets."

Perhaps not all users of the suffix -ess delimit the
qualities of greatness in such labels. It appears that the
term "chiefess" was used in Hawaii with complete casualness
by the islanders.[105] And when Nicholson revised and added
to the material by Fowler on English usage, she argued for
keeping the "feminine designations" and elevating the positions.
If one could measure the rebellion against such labels today,
one might conclude that this position has not been effective.
Or better still, it perhaps depends on the dialect of English.
In Scotland the suffix appears to have wider use and occurs
in such forms as clerkess and manageress. Magnificent

vocalic feats result from pluralizing these forms: clerkesses
and manageresses! A baffling inconsistency in the use of the
suffix -ess is found in the group of nouns: prowess, largess,
and duress. [106]

Syntactic constructions, which involve the putting together of the vocabulary inventory of any language, seem to
have more distinctions of female usage in English than morphological constructions. Females make more use of intensifiers, the often-emphasized words such as: "so, such,
quite, vastly." "It was so interesting." "I had such fun."
Jespersen [107] gives other examples in German, French,
Danish, and Russian, and one wonders if this might not be
a feature of Indo-European language habits.

The way people describe things exhibits male and female characteristics of language use. Several students of
mine have done small studies on the use of adjectives in
male/female linguistic behavior. [108] The conclusions invariably pointed to differences in the use of commonly-known
adjectives. The results fall in the realm of tendency and
avoidance, as with intonation patterns, rather than all-or-
none situations. Women tended to use reduplicated forms
such as "teeny-tiny, itsy-bitsy." They also tended to use
words which emphasized femininity, such as "adorable, bub-
bly, cuddly, cute, darling, exquisite, pretty, precious, and
sweet." They tended to use more emphatic forms such as
"fantastic, horrifying, startling."

Males tended to use forms which emphasized masculinity: "barbed, bristly, leathery, lusty." One notes immediately that the studies showed nothing of varying linguistic
behavior that has to do with linguistic ability, i. e., ability
to innovate creative expressions, to originate complicated
structures, and to correctly use embedded structures. Rather the studies just confirmed role identification and expression of femininity and masculinity.

Besides the differences that males and females exhibit
in their use of adjectives, there is the matter of how people
describe themselves and the other sex. It is not a bit surprising that they tend to describe themselves in terms of
society's description of feminine and masculine patterns. One
senses the frustration of the vicious circle. [109]

The modal construction is another syntactic device
that appears to be prominent in women's speech. When

speakers refer to the kinds of action and the possibilities,
probabilities, and doubtfulness of events that did or will take
place, in English they use the modal class of words--such
as can, could, shall, should, will, would, may, might--
along with other verb auxiliaries, have and been. Females use
more of these words which show indefiniteness, inconclusive-
ness, and uncertainty. Males use less of these words and
their speech tends to be more definite and authoritative (not
necessarily correct!).

There are other uses of these forms which show attitude toward a situation or person. An interesting example occurred recently on a TV newscast, where a manager was being
interviewed about the employment situation in view of the recent
focus on encouraging women to advance to higher status. He
said, "It is very possible that we will have to integrate our present staff ... which we are very pleased to do" (emphasis mine).
Great conflict showed up in the linguistic use of "have to," which
he then tried to nullify by adding that they were "pleased" to be
forced to do this.

Another construction which lends itself to indefinite
and tentative styles of speech is the tag question, [110] a shortened question added to a declarative statement. "He's coming tomorrow, isn't he?" If the information is definitely
known, it can be expressed by the statement alone. Women
tend to add the tag question, not because of lack of information, but to reinforce the feminine image of dependency and
the desire not to appear aggressive and forward. Some observers of the scene have noted that at least some women
frequently use combinations of words such as: what, how,
who, why, with the form "ever" in sentences such as, "Whatever are you doing?" "Whoever would want to do that?"
"However shall I carry all three packages?"

The imperative construction is another indicator of
male /female speech. In a world where women do not usually function in roles of decision-making and giving commands,
it is not surprising that females use alternatives to the imperative construction, which is the simple, direct way of
ordering an action: "Bring that here!" "Write that down!"
"Have my suit cleaned!" Women use constructions which
are not so abrupt and straightforward. Questions substitute
for commands: "Would you drop this by the cleaners on your
way?" Modals soften the approach: "You could include that
in the paragraph if you like." Longer sentences eliminate
brusqueness which is not permitted in feminine speech: "Would
it be all right with you if you had the students turn in these

forms by Friday?" Hortative constructions relieve a woman
from commanding a male figure: "Do let's go!"[111]

It was said that during Sissy (Frances) Farenthold's
campaign, one of her aides needed an ashtray and asked her
to get it. She did, before she realized that it was she who
was supposed to be giving the orders--not taking them. English, of course, is not the only language where sex-differentiated speech is exemplified by command performance. A
study which analyzed the speech of Luo, a language of Kenya,
shows "that the speech of adults, especially males, to young
girls has a higher percentage of imperatives than speech to
boys of comparable ages."[112]

The last example that I wish to set forth here in this
discussion of grammatical constructions is not from the speech
of everyday, ordinary speakers, as the previous examples
have been observed. Rather this is from the writing of the
immortal Virginia Woolf. As so many literary critics have
pointed out, the characters of Woolf's novels, as well as her
other writings, often exemplify the male-female situation in
real life. Mrs. Ramsay, of To the Lighthouse, is the prototype of the wife who is everything else to her family around
her. The oblivious Mr. Ramsay is the prototype of the husband,
the subject of the relationships in the household, in the way
which de Beauvoir so often spoke of in the subject-object
dependency. Mrs. Ramsay typifies the subordinate relation,
the object of the action around her. Heilbrun noticed a remarkable sentence construction in Woolf's writing (emphasis
added):

> And Mrs. Ramsay, in a sentence of significant syn-
> tax, turns out to have died, leaving Mr. Ramsay
> with his arms empty: 'Mr. Ramsay, stumbling
> along a passage one dark morning, stretched his
> arms out, but Mrs. Ramsay having died rather sud-
> denly the night before, his arms though stretched
> out, remained empty.' Mr. Ramsay, the subject
> of this sentence, stretches out his arms which re-
> main empty, the same action which followed his
> desire to be told she loved him, the same distress
> which followed his seeing the stern look on her face
> when he looked into the intricacy of the hedge.
> Mrs. Ramsay exists only in a subordinate clause,
> the object of his needs. [113]

Semantic

In the first chapter we began to discuss categories
and the development of these conceptual categories among
human beings. Grammatical categories are an outgrowth of
the human being's concept of reality, and these classifications
may be true to the facts of nature, or they may be distorted
and not in accord with the facts of nature. People classify
things into categories by characteristics and function. Physical characteristics are used to classify such things as gases,
liquids, and solids, colors, shapes, and sizes. Functional
behavior is used to classify occupations, supernatural beings,
government documents, and women and children. Cross-
cultural examination of how people classify things is an enlightening exercise in people's world-view. For example,
the sun is masculine in Spanish and feminine in German,
and the moon is masculine in German and feminine in
Spanish. In Algonkin the words for raspberry, kettle, and
knee occur in the class of animate gender, and the words
for strawberry, bowl, and elbow occur in the inanimate gender.

Likewise the concept of plural and singular may be
treated in different ways. Rice is singular, but oats are
plural. Is a crowd singular or plural? In the United States
"the government is ..." but in Great Britain "the government
are...." Linguistic classification is sometimes arbitrary;
nevertheless, it is these abstract structures that make a person accept, on the one hand, "The child was frightened" and
reject, on the other hand, "The table was frightened." Another curious example is a bit more subtle: a man can have
children, but only a woman can have babies. The relationship of conceptual categories to everyday behavior is still a
moot question. In some instances they are ignored; people
probably don't think of rice being different in kind from oats.
In other instances they are of supreme importance--super-
natural categories can demand extreme behavior from human
beings. And the sex categories deeply penetrate the value
system and permitted/prohibited behavior of male and female--
certainly far more than is justified by actual physical and
functional differences.

In discussions of structures of languages, semantics
comprises an area which is by far the least understood in
linguistic theory. Jespersen[114] spoke of notional categories
and extralingual categories. He noted that some of them

relate to such facts of the world without as sex, and others
to mental states or to logic. He said, "It will be the gram-
marian's task in each case to investigate the relation between
the notional and the syntactic categories." He then attempted
a "systematic review of the chief notional categories insofar
as they find grammatical expression, and [an] investigat[ion
of] the mutual relation of these two 'worlds' in various languages." Whorf, in the 1930's, also spoke of categories
which marked word classes. He noted certain types of
patterning, or linguistic configurations, which he called lexical selection. He believed that meaning should be stated in
terms of the semantic facts linked with the configurations. [115]

Nevertheless, a generation later, there is still not a
consensus among linguists whether the roles of syntax and
of semantics should be handled as an integrated system or
as separate entities. Therefore, categories such as animacy,
number, status (honorifics), proximacy/distance, dimension
(length, area, volume), and penetrableness (gas, liquid, solid)
are handled in different ways by modern theorists, and sometimes they are not handled at all. Even though it is yet to
be decided whether selectional restrictions are definable in
terms of the restraints of syntax alone, or of syntax and
semantics in conjunction with one another, it is still possible
to make some statements about gender and sex in language
and the relationship between grammars and verbal behavior.

In this study I am making a sharp distinction between
gender and sex. For purposes of distinguishing, I will use
the terminology feminine and masculine to refer to gender,
and male and female to refer to sex. This idea is not new.
In Jespersen's The Philosophy of Grammar, published in 1924,
a chapter is titled "Sex and Gender." Royen's study of 1930
also distinguished sex and gender. In this immense work,
incidentally, Royen gives the history of all theories concerning grammatical gender in Indo-European. More recently,
linguist-philosophers in dealing with the structure of a semantic theory also differentiate between gender and sex. The
semantic markers, Male and Female, are distinguished from
the grammatical markers, which, in a given language, would
be gender distinctions. [116] Recent descriptions of language do
not always make it clear whether gender is to be considered
apart from sex distinctions. Some scholars refer to "mas-
culine/feminine" and some refer to "male/female," without
making the distinction that one set of terms might apply to
gender and another to sex.

In any case, there seem to be three ways of handling
the notion of the division of human beings.   Langendoen[117]
represents one way of treating the sex/gender attributes.
He uses the binary features with a plus or minus Masculine.
Thus [+ Masculine] refers to males and [- Masculine] refers
to females.   McCawley [117] in his proposal for the role of
semantics in a grammar, uses [+male] and [-male], though
with a different position regarding semantics.   He believes
that only semantic information plays a role in selection.
Postal[117] includes only the Masculine feature in his analysis
of English pronouns.   One might conclude that the plus/minus
analysis is good Freud, but not necessarily adequate description.

Another way of treating the semantic distinction of
sex is to consider that both of the features, male and female,
are a positive condition, and both are given autonomous status
and treated as independent wholes.   Katz and Fodor postulate
both male and female as semantic markers.   Jacobs and
Rosenbaum [117] use two plusses in their feature analysis:
⟨+masculine⟩ ⟨+ feminine⟩.   Alyeshmerni and Taubr [117]
describe man and woman with a [+ male] and a [+ female]
feature, respectively.   In explanation of their position, they
say that the [+ male] analysis

> defines woman as 'an adult human being without
> maleness,' but it says nothing, for instance, about
> the fact that a woman has female reproductive or-
> gans and not simply an absence of male reproduc-
> tive organs.   We could define '-male' as '+ female,
> but this would be an ad hoc definition.   It would
> not simplify the grids of such groups as child, pup,
> kitten, and fawn.   To avoid the ad hoc definition,
> one must make female a feature here, as well as
> male. [117]

Gruber [117] also considers that the condition female leads an
existence of its own.   In this consideration, he also presents
a different theoretical approach to selectional features.   Gruber suggests "underlying categorial trees" rather than feature
matrices in his paper on the "functions of the lexicon in formal descriptive grammars."   He suggests "specificatory categories" vs. "contrastive features" in describing lexical items.
Gruber makes an important empirical claim, and says further

> that there should never be a need to call for or
> specify a word by its lack of some quality (for

example, non-human, non-concrete, or non-mass).
The existence of one feature does not necessitate
the existence of some other feature contrastive to
it.

For example, feminine (in the semantic sense)
is not the absence of masculine or even the necessary complement of masculine. It is not a linguistic principle that there be two sexes, nor does the
existence of one of the sexes necessitate (as a linguistic principle) the existence of the other. We
can have them both independently, yet mutually exclusively, generated in the base. [117]

A third way of treating the category of sex in grammars
is to follow the conclusions drawn from human embryological
development, which we have already mentioned in the first
chapter. Thus, [+ female] would be considered basic and
the male would be [- female]. This analysis has never been
suggested in any grammar book or linguistic discussion, but,
as can readily be seen, has more basis in fact than either
of the previous models of analysis.

It is clear that biology is behind certain language
structures in unambiguous ways. For example, the person
that is pregnant is most certainly female (unless he is a
seahorse, my son tells me), and the one who shaves his
beard is most certainly male. There are, however, other
conceptual categories which reflect male and female images
in language. The following illustrate these constraints.

Men bellow; women purr. Men yell; women scream
(or squeal).

... vivacious women, but not vivacious men. ...

Women fret (a recent newspaper headline); men get
angry.

Men have careers; women have jobs. [118]

Married women engage in "homemaking"; single women "keep house."

The concept formation behind the construction of language expressions such as these is a result of learned categories.
Bruner, Goodnow, and Austin, in a book called A Study of
Thinking, [119] speak of "the invention of categories." They
explain that:

> To one raised in Western culture, things that are
> treated as if they were equivalent seem not like
> man-make classes but like the products of nature....
> But there exists a near infinitude of ways of group-
> ing events in terms of discriminable properties,
> and we avail ourselves of only a few of these.

In an appendix to the same book Roger Brown says, "I should
expect all such semantic categories to be susceptible of functional definition by the method of contextual probabilities.
Indeed, I think functional categories are suggested to us by
semantic categories. "

    In my interest and study during the last few years of
Boas', Whorf's, and Sapir and Swadesh's[120] "grammatical
categories," and more recently the "selectional restrictions"
and "groupings" of exponents of transformational theory, I
have become intrigued with the groupings in which women
occur. The following illustrations of such groupings were
collected at random from a great variety of sources of both
written and spoken language. It seems that consideration of
these groupings might throw light on the semantic constraints
behind such constructions as those previously illustrated in
noun-verb and noun-adjective combinations. These notional
categories or selectional groups are powerful forces behind
the actual expressions of language and are based on distinctions which are not regarded as trivial by the speakers of
the language.

    The first examples are from very early times. Rob-
ert Cawdry published A Table Alphabeticall in 1604, saying
that he had gathered the words "for the benefit and helpe of
Ladies, Gentlewomen, or any other unskilfull persons.... "
Another dictionary of 1623 classed women with "young schol-
lars, clarkes, merchants, as also strangers of any nation. "
Thomas Blount intended his Glossographie in 1656 for "the
more knowing women and less-knowing men. "[121] A more
recent scholar was quoted in the AAUP Bulletin--President
Nathan Pusey of Harvard--who, realizing that the draft was
going to reduce the number of men in graduate school, lamented, "We shall be left with the blind, the lame, and the
women. " A famous comedian is known to be vocal about his
"scotch, horses, and ladies. " An editorial starts out naming everything that is rampant these days: "crime, violence,
sex, and women. "

    The Xth Commandment was written for men--(were

women not considered part of the audience?)--they were admonished not to covet their neighbor's: 'house, wife, man-
servant, maidservant, ox, ass, property." The publisher of
the Encyclopaedia Britannica discusses Contract Law and
lists the parties who are not legally competent and who enjoy
indulgence of the courts. These persons are: minors, the
mentally incapacitated, and sometimes special groups such
as married women, convicts, and aliens. In earlier times,
the state of New York once worded its franchise law to include everyone but women, minors, convicts, and idiots.
Often women have been classed with slaves and children. In
Africa secret associations have been formed to keep the women and children in subjection. In Islamic countries, there
are signs on the mosques which instruct, "Women and dogs
and other impure animals are not permitted to enter. "

In Martin's article on the "Speech Levels in Japan
and Korea, "[122] he notes linguistic differences in situations
of address and terms of politeness in the following situations:
women to men, young to old, lower classes to upper classes.
Note that the category comprises women, youth, lower classes.
In the Bengali language women are classed with the children
and the uneducated. Jespersen lists the persons who speak
Sanskrit: gods, kings, princes, brahmans, ministers, cham-
berlains, dancing-masters, other men in superior positions,
and a very few women of special religious importance. Those
who are destined to speak Prakrit are: men of inferior class,
like shopkeepers, law officers, aldermen, bathmen, fishermen, policemen, and nearly all women.

Returning to this country and to more recent times,
one notes that Women's Liberation has engendered new classifications. A recent newspaper article noted the following
group in a news event: Women's Lib people, the Third
World people, the Blacks, the Chicanos. An article in Saturday Review this year referred to a certain crusader as a
"defender of both forms of homosexuality, of Mozart, women's
rights, and dumb animals. " A Fantastic Foster Fenwick
cartoon in the Los Angeles Times grouped the following mar-
chers together: "Women's Lib, Teen Age Lib, Pre-Teen Lib,
Toddlers' Lib. " One of California's bourgeois sea communities prides itself in living a life "dedicated to boats, broads,
and booze. " Section 415. 5 of the Penal Code in California
states that anyone can be arrested for using "vulgar, profane
or indecent language within the presence or hearing of women
or children...."

In discussing the impact and potency of words in their creative effect, a famous anthropologist says, "You utter a vow or you forge a signature and you may find yourself bound for life to a monastery, a woman or a prison." Spiro Agnew added to the collection of groupings that include women in a speech on August 26, 1970, "Women's Liberation Day." His remarks were something to the effect that it is difficult to tame "oceans, fools, and women."

That's how women are categorized. It's as simple as that. Paradoxically, the reasons for it are at the same time profoundly complex and the implications are deeply embedded in the thinking and subsequent behavior of human beings in their own actions and in the interrelatedness of human beings. Of all the grammatical/behavioral categories, probably no concept so determinedly governs human behavior.

Chapter IX

SPEAKING IN REFERENCE
TO MALE AND FEMALE

Every language has a set of forms with which reference is made to people or things that are the focus of discussion. These referents may be known and previously specified or they may be unknown or non-specific. "Mrs. Brown"
will be referred to as "she"; unspecified people may be referred to as "they." We have already considered some of
the ways in which people can be referred to, for example,
titles and names. Here we can expand our discussion and
deal directly with pronominal forms and nominals. The
pronominal forms in English, "I, you, he, she, it, we, they, "
belong to a "closed" class of linguistic forms. There are
only seven, and over the centuries the inventory of this class
is not likely to change, even though other changes take place
every generation or so. Of course, circumstances can
emerge which can change this class--dropping or gaining
some forms. In the last few hundred years, for example,
the forms "thou" and "thee" have been dropped. The form
"they" was added with the Scandinavian invasions many centuries ago.

If one compares the English set of forms with similar
pronominals in other languages, different situations come to
light. Spanish has ten forms: "yo, tu, Vd., el, ella, noso-
tros, nosotras, Vds., ellos, ellas." The matter of declar-
ing sex of referent is required, not only of the "he-she"
referent, but also of the "we" and "they." Another dimension is added--that of status or degree of familiarity. In
speaking to a person of close relationship, the form is "tu";
to a person of more formal relationship, the form is "Vd. "
and both of these are simply translated "you" in English. All
the Indo-European languages use some of these same dimensions in their sets of pronouns--no two languages are exactly alike in their use of referents, but there are similarities
which have derived from a common mother tongue.

Other languages of the world may require that other
dimensions be declared in the pronominals. In some languages the pronoun "we" has forms that indicate whether "we"
includes only two persons (dual) or whether it includes more
than two (plural). Still again, "we" may have to indicate
whether only those persons present are included or whether
persons absent from the scene are also--inclusive and exclusive forms. Some languages have an extensive range of
honorifics in the pronoun system. Aztec has a form "yejwa"
which corresponds to our "he-she-it" with no regard for gender or sex, but it can be used with an honorific "yejwatsin"
which means "honorable he-she-it." It is used for God,
Chief, and a highly respected person. In practice, the "it"
would not occur with an honorific because this kind of honor
is attributed only to animate beings. The Thai language has
the possibility of adding honorific forms even to the first
person "I"--which indicates status relationships between the
persons speaking.

The matter of possession at times and in some languages changes pronoun referent. We might use a nonpersonal "it" for a nonpersonal thing--e.g., "its toy"; "her"
(or "his") might be used for personal body parts of a baby--
when referring, for example, to "her hair." In English,
body parts co-occur with a personal possessive pronoun--
"wash your hands",--but in Spanish the pronoun is impersonal
and not possessive: "lave las manos" (wash the hands). The
context of situation makes it perfectly clear that the hands
belong to the person addressed. The possessive pronoun, on
the other hand, is used with impersonal objects: "traiga su
libro" (bring your book).

Besides possession, personal and gender reference is
often intertwined with animate/inanimate concepts. These
ideas go back long before history was recorded and we can
only speculate on the origins, and on the contemporary situations that have derived from earlier thinking. "Mother
Earth" undoubtedly had some spiritually animate qualities in
the belief system of early earth dwellers and it is no great
surprise to note that the land often is referred to as "she."
Even though many ideas have been lost in the shuffle of civi-
lizing people and their thinking, remnants remain. Another
thing to consider in analyzing our English use of he/she for such
things as ideas and animals and objects is the proto-language
backgrounds. We often refer to dogs as "he" and cats as
"she" and various explanations have been attempted which
have to do with size of animal and temperament. It might be

e

noted that in German "der Hund" (dog) belongs to the masculine gender classification and "die Katz" (cat) belongs to the
feminine gender. It is not unlikely that the influence of our
Germanic heritage has caused present-day English often to
maintain that gender distinction in reference.

It is clear from these and countless examples that can
be observed daily that the matter of gender and sex referents
is intricately mixed with other behavioral categories and linguistic dimensions. The English pronoun system is a rather
simple system in comparison with other languages of the
world, as far as the forms are concerned. Only seven forms
are possible, thus not many choices have to be made regarding such things as sex, honorific, familiarity, presence or
absence, distance. Most of the time the grammatical forms
of language correspond to the realities of nature. For example, in the sentence, "The boy hurt himself," gender markers
and sex coincide. In fact, there are so many examples such
as this in English, that we are lulled into the comfortable
thinking that all is well and regular. In fact, the pronoun
system in English is inadequate to handle many things that
we want to say, where at times we need ambiguity, or some
way to make reference to non-specific persons. The following examples illustrate this lack:

> Someone tried to get in, didn't (he, she, they)?
> Someone owes you money, doesn't (she, he)?
> Someone's knocking, (aren't, isn't) (he, she, they)?
> One of us could go, couldn't (I, you, we)?

Whorf also gave examples of the inconsistent use of pronouns
in English (Whorf had two goldfish, Jane and Dick):

> Each goldfish likes its food.
> *Jane likes its food better than Dick.
> *Tom [a dog] came out of its kennel.
> My baby enjoys its food.
> *My baby's name is Helen--see how Helen enjoys its
>   food.
> *My little daughter enjoys its food.
> That's Boston--*I live in it. [123]

The use of the editorial we is another example of inconsistency in pronoun referent. Mark Twain commented that "Only
presidents, editors, and people with tapeworm have the right
to use the editorial 'we'."

If all the categories and dimensions that are possible
were used in a language it would be intolerably cumbersome.
Therefore languages filter out some possibilities and mixes
and are inevitably asymmetrical at some points.   It is this
that causes ambiguity at times, not only in the linguistic
system, but in the communication processes between human
beings.   Nevertheless, ambiguity is a necessary and useful
device in language and a powerful and intriguing device for
poets.   Interpersonal relationships are maintained by ambiguity, where either a lie or an absolute truth would destroy.
An impersonal, ambiguous reference can be tolerated.   To
be practical, people need an ambiguous way of referring to
an unknown person who rang the doorbell, or started gossip,
or fixed the telephone lines, or gave warnings.   An impersonal "they" is often used in expressions in English: "No-
body knows, do they?" "Somebody could hurt themselves."
"Anyone in their right mind...." Shakespeare used this useful combination: "God send everyone their harts desire."

English is at a disadvantage in meeting the need of
an ambiguous, unspecified, unknown person referent.   Languages which have no distinction of male/female for the
third person pronoun, such as Hungarian, Finnish, Aztec, or
Chinese, do not have this problem.   In situations in English
it is often stated that the pronoun "he" is used in a generic
sense to cover both sexes.   Law documents, for example,
are supposed to have this intent in the writings.   In addition
to the pronoun "he," it is also said that the male forms such
as "man" and "mankind" are used as generic terms which
include both male and female.   Jespersen points out that this
interpretation was "a natural linguistic consequence of the
social preponderance during many centuries," and this is
quite believable, although he also noted a growing use of the
term "human".[124] Nowadays this usage is being challenged
on a two-point basis.   People who believe that the condition
"human" outranks the condition of sex are no longer satisfied
with using male terms.   And, more seriously, innumerable
counter-examples show that, indeed, the terms are often used
with no thought of women in mind.   For example, an article
published recently says, "The first of these sections shows
that a man's consistent pronoun style ..." and on the next
page "... describes the ways in which a man may vary his
pronoun style...."   The topic of discussion was not "men"
but pronoun use in general.   A book on academic life is entitled: The Academic Mysteryhouse: The Man, the Campus,
and Their New Search for Meaning.   To add insult to injury,
in the acknowledgments, the author says that his wife and

secretary helped write, edit, type, and revise the book!

Many of these counter-examples are offensive, but this "generic rule" can also lead to absurdities. A recent research report discusses "the development of the uterus in rats, guinea pigs and men." Perhaps a wish to develop a new species? And these absurdities make a farce of law. [125] This year a county judge in Indiana threw out of court a charge made against a female dancer. It had to do with indecent exposure, but the judge pointed out that the law specifically refers to a person exposing an inappropriate part of his body. Another state has a law which reads, "No person may require another person to perform, participate in or undergo an abortion of pregnancy against his will."

If the use of "he" were the linguistic convenience that it is said to be, then one would be unable to find counter-examples where shifting of pronoun takes place within the dialogue, or where "he" and "she" are used exclusively for certain categories of people. Certain occupational roles are invariably designated with a single gender: policeman, doctor, bricklayer, president, sailor, and professor are "he"; nurse, elementary teacher, secretary, baby-sitter, typist, and housekeeper are "she." A computer count of the occurrence of words in children's reading material showed that "he" is used three times as much as "she" in the writings. [126] This is a reflection of culture, not of linguistic structures but should be noted in terms of acquisition of language and role patterns. Also, I have noted elsewhere, [127] that in children's books animals are almost always referred to as "he" except when the animals are objects of derision such as the fat sow who entered the Fat Pigs contest, and the mother duck with "the bold ferocious mien," or when they carry names of derogation, such as Petunia the Goose or Frances the Badger. Interestingly enough, one of the Bantu languages uses the feminine "mother" prefix with animals in a mocking sense: mother-hyena, mother-goose, mother-porcupine. [128]

The "generic rule" is never observed for teachers in the lower grades. Unspecified teachers are referred to as "she" although it does seem to be applied to levels above high school. A poem about professors in a recent AAUP Bulletin used the masculine referents entirely, along with the nominal referent "a man." As quoted in the student newspaper, a regent of a well-known university referred to the faculty as "a distinguished group of men...." A significant reversal of the rule that masculine referents are used for

non-specific persons occurred in a term paper turned in to
me last year.   The antecedent was "a student" and the following referent was "she."   Perhaps this student had just
heard the joke going around the country concerning God.
When asked to describe God, the informant replies, "Well,
to begin with, she's Black!"

One of the most curious examples that I have collected comes from an up-tight etiquette book of the 1930's, which
has quaint little chapters on how to behave.   Chapter 14 is
called "The Sniffler and the Snorter" and refers to the un-
identified offender by shifting back and forth between "he"
and "she" (emphasis added):

> There is no cure.   Have pity on her.   Sometimes
> it is he who sniffles.   It makes no difference.   If
> you beg her to stop, she will continue.   If you ask
> him to stop, he will never call again.   (That would
> be just too bad.)
>   Don't tell your friend that he sniffles, because
> he won't believe you.   You are the only one who
> ever accused him of such a thing, and while he's
> telling you this he sniffles and doesn't even know
> it.   The person who snorts when she laughs is
> also out of order.   There is nothing disgusting a-
> bout this habit but the sound is unpleasant.   Watch
> your laugh and see if you snort. [129]

This pronoun shifting in less deliberate circumstances
reflects conceptual structures.   At times the shifts are status defined.   In a planning session for a new project on a
university campus, there occurred a noticeable shift in the
pronoun referents to the hypothetical personnel who were to
be employed.   When the decision-making personnel were referred to, the pronoun was invariably he; when the personnel
at the level of secretary were referred to, the pronoun was
invariably she.   Written material adds to these examples.
A book on teaching reading informs the reader, "When the
teacher attempts to overcome the first kind of ignorance ...
she discovers that the student shows a strong and inexpli-
cable resistance to learning the few simple rules that he
needs to know."   Another book from the field of education
refers to both the researcher and the teacher (emphasis added):   "The psycholinguist sometimes tries to bridge the gap
between what he can legitimately conclude....   The teacher
may believe that an object is blue, but if she accepts...."
Very recent examples which occur in only isolated places,

use only that "she" form: "It gives the reader all the back-
ground she needs.... " This seems to be in the spirit of
experimentation or facetiousness.

In view of the ability to switch between he and she
among English speakers, in spite of what the rule books say,
the next illustration is shocking to the point of comedy (emphasis added):

The Secret
We have a secret, just we three,
The robin, and I, and the sweet cherry tree; ...
But of course the robin knows it best,
Because he built the--I shan't tell the rest;
And laid the four little--something in it--
I'm afraid I shall tell it every minute.
. . .
--Anonymous 130

There are two areas in the analysis of language and
human behavior where the pronoun referent is of particular
interest, and these are religion and medicine. In these two
areas, in any culture of the world, women are essential and
often predominant participants in the scene. In spite of that,
quotations such as the following are not uncommon:

The schizophrenic is desperate, is simply without
hope. I have never known a schizophrenic who
could say he is loved, as a man .... When someone says he is an unreal man or that he is dead....

First among the classification of silences is the
silence of the pure listener, of womanly passivity;
... [another is] the silence of indifference.... This
is the ominous silence of the wife who woodenly
listens to her husband relating the little things he
so earnestly wants to tell her.... There is no
greater distance than that between a man in prayer
and God.

Mary Baker Eddy, the founder of Christian Science, apparently
had a more androgynous approach in her philosophy of religion.
She recommended that the participants use the form "Mother
Father Creator" in their prayers.

It would appear from these anecdotal observations that
the grammatical rules often cited for the use of personal gender

are a fiction and that actual use does not corroborate the
stated rules.   There is a need for careful studies on the use
of gender to clarify what the real situation is in this uneasy
adjustment between language and culture.   Simone de Beauvoir
points out another type of pronoun referent that results from
the larger issue of how females are regarded and how they
regard themselves.   Women do not use the referent "we,"
except, for instance, in formal circumstances at a meeting;
other groups do have a solidarity that produces the "we" when
they refer to their condition.   Negroes, Portuguese fishermen,
Swedish immigrants, the wealthy, educators, and all such
groups regard themselves as subjects, in contrast to the "others" out there.   But females are not the Subject.   He is the
subject--father, husband, son--and she is the Other.   So
there is no solidarity of "we" with a unified strength.   De
Beauvoir first put forth these ideas in 1949.   There has, of
course, been some change since then.

The pronoun "it" is full of intrigue. [131]   The referent
is cursorily described as a single inanimate object, but it is
much more complex than that.   "It" may have an antecedent,
but may be used as a euphemism without an explicit antecedent, for such things as urine and outhouse.   In fact, I remember seeing an old outhouse at a service station on one
of the highways across the desert of the Southwest which was
named "It."   The euphemism was two-fold--the outhouse also
served for both "he" and "she."   It is of interest to note
that a ghost, a dwarf and a corpse are "it"; these illustrations might influence one to choose the diagram from the
first chapter showing the quality "humanness" in the higher
node--that is, the human feature is in the hierarchy above
either male or female.

In former times, it was not uncommon for human beings to be referred to as "it."   Here is an entry from Johnson's dictionary for "Person" (emphasis added):   "A person
is a thinking intelligent being that has reason and reflection
and can consider itself as itself, the same thinking thing in
different times and places."   Though we no longer use "it"
in this way, contemporary English retains some expressions
where the pronoun "it" has human referents.   "Who is it?"
"It is I/It's me."   A group of cognitive verbs co-occur with
"it" as a reference to a human: believe, think, guess, hope,
know, suppose, anticipate, as in "I believe it was John."
Another class of verbs co-occur with "it," such as "seems"
or "appears," as in "It seems it was John."   In these
times of challenging the present pronominal use of "he"

and she, " speakers of English might consider reversing the
trend away from using "it" for an unspecified person and going
back to Johnson's use of "it" for "person--unspecified for sex. "

   The discussion so far has dealt with referents that
were unspecified and the confusion and distortions that result
from not knowing what to say.   There is another group of
interesting phenomena that occur when the referent is known
and able to be specified according to sex.   These are anomalous constructions which occur where the pronoun (or noun)
referent is not the same gender as the known sex of the precedent.   Theorists in linguistics would label this anomaly
"nonobservation of selectional restrictions. "   Sometimes in-
cidents such as these have been simply put aside as "exceptions" in the grammar, or unimportant incidentals.   Scholars
are coming more and more to see that "exceptions" arc the
messy residue of undiscovered facts.

   In the course of studying languages, I have recorded
eight instances where anomalous constructions occur.   First,
non-native speakers have difficulties with the gender system,
particularly the covert system, to use Whorf's terms.   The
difficulty is dependent upon the native language of the speaker.   If the native language has a distinction between "he"
and "she" then the speaker learning English will have little
difficulty.   If the native language is Chinese, or Hungarian,
or Aztec, then the speaker will often be heard referring to
a woman as "he" or to a man as "she. "   An unusual example
was articulated by an Italian woman who spoke English fairly
well.   It should be remembered here that Italian also has
differentiated "he" and "she. "   In a review of a book which
was written by another Italian woman, the speaker consistently
referred to the author as "he. "   At the coffee hour later,
she explained the discrepancy, "Well, you just expect a scholar to be a man!"

   Second, in certain dialects of Black English in such
regions as coastal South Carolina, Georgia, and Florida,
children especially will use anomalous forms. [132]

>   He a nice little girl
>   Here he book (referring to hers)
>   Here come he boyfriend (referring to hers)

It is very likely that these forms are based on very old patterns brought from Africa centuries ago, where the languages
there do not differentiate between male and female in the

pronoun system.   Nevertheless, this is somewhat different
from the speakers who are learning English in this generation.
The third instance is child language, that is, the speech of
the period of the acquisition of language.   When a youngster is learning to talk, he or she has not yet learned to
control all the grammatical categories and may refer to Daddy as "she" and Mommy as "he", in addition to mixing up
the "it" and personal referent.   The fourth instance occurs
in the language of homosexuals.   The pronoun "she" may be
used to designate certain men with "female" behavior and the
pronoun "he" may be used for certain women with "male"
behavior.

        The fifth instance is a form of baby talk.   In the
Marathi language of India a form of endearment is indicated
by a variety of baby talk which switches gender referents.
"The use of masculine ending and/or concord for a girl's
name, of feminine ending and/or concord for a boy's name,
and of neuter ending and/or concord for both"[133] shows
endearment.   A similar situation exists in Arabic.   For example, "wēn ruhti yā binti?" (Where did you go [fem.], little girl?) said to a boy: and "inta žu'ān?" (Are you [masc.]
hungry [masc.] ?) said to a girl.   In English we sometimes
hear "it" used in baby talk: "Did it hurt itself?"[134] This
anomaly in baby talk and endearment is strangely paralleled
in an opposite meaning, that of insult and denigration.   The
famous linguist Jakobson cites examples from the Russian
language where the feminine gender applied to a male is
used in expressive, pejorative language.[135]   Other Russian
scholars have noted this form of insult to a man.[136]   You
don't just call him an "idiot"--you call him a "female idiot"
(the English translation is awkward.)   A similar kind of insult is possible in the Czech language.[137]   And Marathi,
which uses the switching for endearing baby talk, may use
it for contempt in adult speech.

        Studies of English dialects note that "she" may be
used contemptuously when referring to a man.[138]   Long ago
in Scotland, the men from the Highland clans insulted their
chief by calling him a "Hen Chief" when they thought his
conduct would not become a real man.[139]   More recently,
a literary scholar notes that Norman Mailer uses a similar
device for showing contempt: "Croft's most withering insult
is to castigate his subordinates as "a pack of goddam wom-
en."[140]   In addition to the feminine reference, another form of
insult is to dehumanize the person by using the pronoun "it."
Webster's Third gives examples such as "just listen to it

talk" "just look at my daddy and the big car it has."[141]

 The seventh instance of anomaly is a deliberate inconsistency of pronoun referent used for effect by comedians.
On a TV program heard recently, the audience responded
with laughter to the comedian who was telling about a tiger:
"The tiger's name is Sarah. Isn't he nice?" The last example of mismatch occurs in languages with grammatical
gender, when the gender of the noun conflicts with the gender
of the person. In French, for example, le docteur is masculine gender, but may refer to a woman. Linguistic writings have great fun with the French professor who is pregnant! "Le professeur (masculine gender) est enceinte." Jespersen, who speaks of these anomalies as "incongruities"
cites several humorous examples. [142] A conversation about
an ape is taken from Swedish: "Hvad heter den här apan?
--Hon heter Kalle, för det är en hanne." What is the name
of that ape? She is called Charles, for it is a he. (In
Swedish apa is feminine.) A Spanish lover becomes a comic
when he wants to tell his sweetheart that she is an angel.
In Spanish "angel" is masculine gender, and there is no way
to reconcile the grammatical concord with a female. "Ella
es como un ángel."

 The preceding discussion and examples have to do with
reference to human beings. Another area of significance is
the matter of personal referent to an inanimate object or to
an abstract idea. [143] Why do we refer to a little red sports
car and to justice as "she" and to Old Man River as "he"?
This situation can only occur in languages with feminine and
masculine genders. It seems to be highlighted in English
where nonhuman nouns do not carry grammatical gender, in
contrast to other Indo-European languages where every table,
window, tree, and river has a masculine or feminine referent according to the grammatical form. This is an especially delicate matter when it comes to translations between the
languages. Jespersen and Jakobson relate some examples of
the difficulties. [144] Shakespeare's passage, "See how the
morning opes her golden gates, And takes her farewell of
the glorious sun," is an image in which the morning is the
mistress who bids farewell to her lover, the sun. In German,
the word "morning" is masculine and "sun" is feminine, so
the translator inverts the relationship. "Sieh, wie sein tor
der goldene morgen öffnet, Und abschied von der lieben
sonne nimmt." That kind of modification is not so difficult.
Translations of Milton into French, however, are seemingly
impossible. Sin is talking to Satan who has begotten on her

his son Death, where "le péché" (sin) is masculine, and
therefore cannot be the mother, and "la mort" (death) is
feminine and cannot be the son.

Vygotsky gives some charming examples of the challenge of coherent translation of nonhuman nominals. [145] The
German poem by Heine about a fir and a palm could not be
translated literally into Russian with the same nuances. The
poem suggests the love of a man for a woman, and in German
fir is masculine and palm is feminine. In Russian both of
these trees are feminine, and so in order to retain the im-
plication, one translator replaced the fir tree by a masculine
cedar. Another translator made a literal translation and
lost the poetic overtones. Vygotsky also relates the problems
of translating the fable "La Cigale et la Fourmi," where La
Fontaine's French grasshopper is feminine and symbolizes a
lighthearted, carefree attitude. In Russian grasshopper is
masculine, so the translator settled for dragonfly, in order
to continue with the thought of the author.

It is not unlikely that these backgrounds of gender personification in Indo-European languages have something to do
with the genders used in English today, even though we have
lost grammatical gender in the sense that French, Russian,
and German continue to use it. What, then, is our situation
in English? Grammar books try to cite the rules in an
orderly fashion. Here is an example:

> In this system [of 'hidden gender distinctions'],
> larger animals are usually 'he,' while smaller
> animals, personified countries or states, nature,
> automobiles, trains, sailboats, and motorboats
> are usually 'she.' In short, power represents
> the masculine, grace the feminine. [146]

In the early 1920's a European scholar made an attempt to find the system of personal gender for inanimate
things in English. [147] He read through hundreds of books
and documented examples from 175 of these. The illustrations are all from men speakers and all of the pronoun referents are the feminine she/her. The characters quoted
are men "with work-calloused hands and speech uninfluenced
by literature"--men from the industries of fur, timber, and
mining, as well as cowboys. The novels dealing with the
upper and middle classes contributed very little to the collection of examples and the conclusion was drawn that there is
a close relation of status of speaker and the use of she for

inanimate objects. This vast study did bring together a few
ideas toward explaining the use of personal gender in referring to inanimate things, such as literary versus colloquial
"homely" style, spoken versus written language, personification of the instrument by the craftsman (the sailor's ship,
the soldier's gun, the driver's car), artifical versus natural
objects, American versus British dialect, foreign language
influence, and emotional characterisitcs of emphatic expressions (she's a dandy!).   Most importantly it was concluded
that the rules of grammar researched in grammar rule books
did not match actual usage, at least in the written language,
and the explanations were dubious.   It seems clear that much
of the confusion has to do with dialects.   An interesting study
would be to investigate these differences by dialects in such
far-spread places as Canada, northern Great Britain, Ireland,
and Australia. 148

   The overwhelming number of examples that I have observed in all the studies I can find, show that the feminine
pronouns are by far the favorites.   Masculine pronouns are
used for: death, hate, and war (horrors!); sometimes for
rivers.   Mountain climbers refer to El Capitan as "he."
This may be because the Spanish word is in masculine gender.   Lewis Carroll, in "The Walrus and the Carpenter," referred to the sun as "he" and the moon as "she."   Does
this show influence from other languages?   And the European
scholar gently chides professors for giving a grammatical
rule for a gentleman's pipe to be referred to as "he"--in
actuality, a man may refer to his pipe as "she".

   In view of the preponderance of feminine referents
for personifications occurring in natural language and in uninhibited situations, it is noteworthy that children's readers
and textbooks do not follow this practice. 149   In these books,
personifications of the inanimate are invariably male.   The
wind, snowman, broom, table and chair are all male.   No
sailor worth his salt in real life would refer to a ship as
"he"; even destroyers named after men ("Patrick Henry")
are referred to as "she."   But our children's boats, ma-
chines, trains, and automobiles carry male names and gender reference.   This kind of ambivalence is sure to produce
some kind of double bind in the child learner.   This discrepancy also forces another kind of evaluation.   The use of
feminine gender in novels might in some cases reflect something about the things talked about, for example, a romantic
view of the Muses, beauty, loyalty, and creativity.   But the
almost total reversal of this in children's books reflects

something of the motivation and goals of the writers and pro-
ducers of the books.   Is education so feminized that it must
frenetically masculinize its books by using male pictures and
male referents?   Will this distortion of language patterns
solve the problem?

In the studies done on personification by using a human gender referent, there is ample evidence that this type
of language falls into the areas of emotive language in both
pleasurable and unpleasurable ways.   Studies done in the
Russian and Czech languages also show a kind of emotive
language expressed by gender referents. [150] An emotionally
colored utterance, for example in Czech, would result in an
anomalous construction, combining masculine and feminine
gender: kluk (m.) hloupá (f.), "a silly boy," and chlap (m.)
špatná (f.), "a bad fellow." It has not been as widely acknowledged in English that personification of this sort is a
kind of expressive, emotive language.   But certainly in many
cases, perhaps most, it is just that.   It has been previously
noted that males predominate in using this pattern of speech.
It has also been noted that the reference is sometimes made
in devotion and endearment, and is sometimes made in anger
or hatred.   e. e. cummings masterfully uses the feminine
referent as he describes, tongue-in-cheek, the adventures of
a man with his first car (his first woman?) in the poem, "she
being Brand. "[151]

Previously we have noted that males do not use the
expressive patterns of emotions in intonation, or in the use
of intensifiers and superlatives, nearly as much as females
do.   It may well be that males find their outlet in·feminine
personification, in addition to the well-recognized release of
swearing.   What we will eventually see, I think, is that both
male and female have emotional language in equal quantities,
and that the devices they use are culturally defined.

Before we summarize our findings-in-flux on the situations of pronominal referents in English, I want to mention
a couple of anecdotes, which, I hope, will help us keep from
taking ourselves too seriously.   A friend of mine has a dentist who personifies teeth by using the gender referent opposite to the sex of the owner.   A tooth of his own the dentist
refers to as "she," and his wife's, as "he."   Another curios-
ity occurs in the French language, and must be the source
of much fun and satire.   The word for love, "l'amour," is
masculine; love-making, "la cour," is feminine; and adultery,
"l'adultère," is masculine.

Tentative Summary of Pronominal Referents in English

Inanimate Gender $\left\{\begin{array}{l}\text{neuter} \\ \text{feminine} \\ \text{masculine}\end{array}\right\}$

> it: machinery, furniture, [euphemism], linguistics...
> they (singular): pants, scissors, clothes...
> she: muse, ship, hurricane...
> he: ???

Animate Sex $\left\{\begin{array}{l}\text{unspecified} \\ \text{female} \\ \text{male}\end{array}\right\}$

> unspecified, singular
> it: baby, child, goldfish, animal...
> she: nurse, elementary teacher, small animal...
> he: doctor, professor, large animal...
> he or she: (recent usage shows more occurrences
>   of this alternative)
> we: (editorial)
> they: someone...

> specified
>   female
>   she, and he for anomalous forms
>   male
>   he, and she for anomalous forms

Nominals belong to another class of words which are used for referents. We have already mentioned the nominals "man" and "mankind" which are said to refer to both sexes in a generic sense. Other words referring to male and female often have to do with occupation or position. The often quoted Fowler's Modern English Usage observed in 1926 that "... with the coming extension of women's vocations, feminines for vocation-words are a special need of the future...." A Russian scholar observes that the Bolshevik Revolution brought about changes which produced a need for new terminology to refer to women occupying certain jobs or positions. [152]

Sexual experiences show a remarkable use of reference. The word "adulterer" on many occasions refers only to the woman--males are not charged with adultery. In Italy the penal and civil codes indicated that the word "adultery" could

legally refer only to women.   "Peeping Tom" is an expression used only for males, though there is no clear scientific
justification for believing that females are not qualified to be
Peeping Toms.   The recent sell-outs of the magazines with
nude male centerfolds attest to that.   If "man/men" is a
term widely used and understood to be meant in a generic
sense, then the following illustration is of significance.   A
newscaster on the radio recently reported a police raid saying, ".. . persons taken in a surprise raid from massage
parlors. "   Why wasn't the generalized "men" used?

Another group of terms and names with sexual reference have to do with topography.   A drive through the country
will bring to attention: Tetons (Teats), Nippletop, Nipple
Peak, Squaw Peak.   Some of the local names are not found
in official documents.   Maiden's Peak is known to the old-
timers as Squaw Tit.   And pilots have redubbed two mountains called Percy Peaks, as the Jane Russell Peaks. [153]
"The Average American" is an expression that should include
both sexes, but definitions which follow the expression preclude any thought of females participating.

During his life, the average American consumes 26
million gallons of water, 10, 000 pounds of meat
and 28, 000 pounds of milk and cream while yearly
junking seven million cars, 100 million tires, 20
million tons of paper, 28 billion bottles and 48
billion cans. .. .   In short, he's quite a man.

For all the elegance of his dress, the richness
and variety of his diet, the horsepower of his motor
cars and the glitter of his women folk, the average
American. .. .

"The Average Shopper, " however, is usually "she. "
This is an economic appeal where linguistics and economics
intertwine.   Here money talks, and the "she" is elevated to
a central and important position.   I have one curious example
that switches the reference to a consumer.   The title says,
"How the consumer can protect herself" and two pages later
the article continues, "The poor customer.   He has a tough
job.   He can't tell a thing. .. . "   It has been argued that the
word "manpower" includes both male and female working
force.   However, when the Boy Scouts of America advertise
that "America's Manpower Begins with Boypower, " it is clear
that females are not considered in the expression.

A very common expression in English uses the word

"man" for groups and committees: "a 12-man committee. "
In a conference I attended recently, the speaker discussed
the organization of a group and referred to "a group of 12
men...." Giggles and objections from the audience inter-
spersed his comments, and the next time, he said, "a group
of men and women. " Adjustments such as these are useful,
until the whole human race realizes that women comprise
half of the population. As a matter of fact, one does hear
the expression "men and women" ever more frequently. Indeed women have come a long way from 1771 when the makers
of the first Encyclopaedia Britannica wrote only six words of
information for the entry "Woman: the Female of Man. See
Homo. "

    Dialogues and all manner of behavior today show that
change is very much in evidence. A friend of mine told me
of an incident with her small son which illustrates this.
One day the youngster came home with all the indications
that he had been the loser in a tough tiff. His mother asked
him if he had hit the kid back, to which he answered, "No,
she ran away!"

Chapter X

STATUS AND STANDARD/NONSTANDARD LANGUAGE

"Women are to be talked to as below men and
above children. "
--Lord Chesterfield[154]

The emphasis on femininity and masculinity has blurred
the caste sytem which prevails in our society.   This is not
a popular theme to discuss and in some bailiwicks it is not
acceptable in any form.   All kinds of restrictions and limitations have been imposed on a female's linguistic habits,
with the idea that these behavioral patterns would ensure her
femininity.   Thus she is not permitted to swear or use
"coarse" language.   She is given titles and respect--males
must not swear in her presence--in countless ways she is
given "better" treatment.   But all of this simply results in
keeping women out of the running.   In order to continue a
caste system it is necessary for those in the lower ranks to
accept their status.   To all outward appearances women have
accepted this lower status, often in the belief that it was
femininity they were perpetuating.   Religious instruction that
this is right and the natural order of things has helped maintain the womanly image.   These are powerful beliefs in the
minds of females who want to be "real ladies" and in the
minds of males who treasure and revere their "true ladies. "

There is evidence in language that this acceptance may
only be a superficial mask overlaying other attitudes or feelings though out-of-awareness.   In linguistic studies there are
many examples of instances where female usage shows an
attempt at "proper" language or more "refined" language.   One
can observe, even within the same family where the rearing
and schooling have been identical, that very often the women
use standard English and the men do not.   We have already
noted the difference of pronunciation in the -ing ending of
verbs, with little girls carefully pronouncing -ing, and the
boys shuffling off with -in. [155]   Other dialects of English have

THE ALUMNAE

"I can't see why you're so insulted at being called a
chick, Magda, — now that chicken is selling at $1.09
a pound."

By Mary Gauerke; copyright © 1973 by The Register and
Tribune Syndicate; reproduced by permission.

---

shown a similar status-sex relationship.   In South Africa,
in the English-speaking universities, the men speak with
more dialect features of South African English than the women, who seem to be more sensitive to the social connotations of dialect. [156]

In a dialect of Great Britain, an extensive study was
done to test the hypothesis that women "consistently produce
linguistic forms which more closely approach those of the
standard language or have higher prestige than those produced
by men, or alternatively, that they produce forms of this
type more frequently. [157]   It was concluded that there is a
very close relationship between sex differences in linguistic
usage and status aspirations.   It would appear, then, that
women have not universally accepted the position in the lower
ranks, and that, out-of-awareness, and in a socially acceptable and non-punishable way, women are rebelling.

These distinctions are not difficult to maintain, on the
other hand, because males, all too often, identify nonstandard
language with masculinity.   How many American families
speaking standard English at home have gone through the trau-
matic experience of their teen-age sons coming home with
double negatives and "he don't's"?   It appears to be general

American tradition that a red-blooded male would rather be caught dead than be grammatical! A recent advertising campaign recognized this and exploited the possibilities. On a huge billboard along one of the freeways into Los Angeles, a cigarette company put up a sign which showed a picture of a young man and a young lady. His statement said, "Winston tastes good like a cigarette should" and her statement said, "Winston tastes good as a cigarette should"! A TV commercial continued the grammatical distinction when the young lady in the commercial corrected her companion's grammar by saying, "You mean as a cigarette should...." Apparently females attempt some kind of equilibrium by reaching a higher status in language to compensate for their lower status as members of society, and males attempt a kind of masculine identity by using language to maintain a group solidarity. Earlier in the century American Speech published a study of "affected and effeminate words" showing that students equated culture and effeminancy. Males, especially, avoided words which fell into these classes. [158]

Status distinctions in language are universal. The degree and use of these distinctions differ from language to language. We have seen that status and sex distinctions are closely related in English. Are they also in other languages? It would seem that they are. In Germany I was told that boys tend to use more "dialect" and girls tend to use "standard" language. In Italian and Spanish, [159] upper-class women are very conscious of their pronunciation with regard to the tongue position and placement in the mouth. "It is considered plebeian and socially inelegant. to have a back articulation, and especially upper-class women affect a very fronted style of articulation. [160]

Jespersen tells of the situation in old Indian drama, where women talk Prakrit (prakrta, the natural or common language) and men talk Sanskrit (samskrta, the adorned language). [161] The principal distinction, however, is rank, not sex. In the discussion of categories we noted that Sanskrit was the language of the upper echelons, and Prakrit was the language of men of inferior classes and nearly all women. Sapir, in his study of the Yana language, suggested that "the reduced female forms constitute a conventionalized symbolism of the less considered or ceremonious status of women in the community." [162] The symbolic use of language with reference to sex is an almost unexplored area of language research by linguists. [163] In Japanese, female speakers are expected to use polite expressions more often than males. [164] Japanese

is a language which incorporates many honorifics in the discourse. The use of these has to do with the people involved
and the role they play. More polite forms are expected in
certain relationships, that is, young to old, lower classes
to upper classes, and women to men.

In the study done on Detroit speech, [165] which was
intended to focus on socio-economic factors, the relation between certain syntactic constructions and status dimensions
was shown to be clear-cut. Multiple negation (double negatives), pronominal apposition ("my brother, he went to the
park"), plurals, possessives, third singular verb inflections
were all investigated as to their frequency and use. It was
shown that females are more sensitive to these indicators
of lower status, and are less likely to use them. Linguists
who do field work have noted that dialect differences and unusual forms of speech may be difficult to elicit from women
who are more socially conscious of being denigrated. Language is one way in which females can better themselves,
even if only in their own image.

Many other studies in the past few years have documented that females in the black communities in the United
States show a marked difference in their control of Standard
English in contrast to the males. [166] It is not clear why
this is so; a complex of reasons probably is involved. Black
females may have occasion to hear and speak more standard
English because of their work as domestics in homes where
standard English is spoken. Black males have acquired
the Power of Words in a style and use of language which is
uniquely their own. This versatility and creativity in language is enhanced in a world which is devoid of material
evidence of their power. Thus, masculinity is signaled by
their very special use of language in the way of verbal duel-
ing, playing the dozens, and reciting epics. This is not the
same language which is found in school and in reading mate-
rials--the undesirable effeminate world. But desirable in
another sense--the economic sense. Thus, the young male
struggles with an ambivalence that is seemingly insolvable--
to maintain his masculinity and prowess among his peers, or
to learn the "feminized" language of the mainstream community.

Analogies between the situation of women and black
people have often been made, especially in the last generation since Myrdal's now famous Appendix to his An American
Dilemma. [167] Webster's definition of "disadvantage" applies

to both: "The state or fact of being without advantage: an unfavorable, an inferior, or prejudicial condition." 168   In interpreting male and female differences in any language, it is important to recognize hierarchies of status as well as male/female patterns.   It is well to recognize these aspects of the communication systems and the linguistic demands of these systems, as people either do or do not participate equally in the mainstream of society.

Chapter XI

NONVERBAL, EXTRA-LINGUISTIC MESSAGES [169]

Besides language, there are other ways that people communicate. These extra-linguistic systems are sometimes [170] referred to as nonverbal communication or as body language. There is not yet a unified, widely-understood terminology even though these aspects of communication have been recognized and discussed since classical times. Generally speaking, the things that people do in conveying nonverbal messages fall into two categories: vocalizations and movements. Paralanguage [171] comprises all extra-speech sounds or modifications of speech. There may be separate sounds such as whistling, yelling, or "tsk-tsk." Paralanguage may also consist of modifying features accompanying speech in the way of quality of voice, pitch, loudness--vocal expressions that add emotional and attitudinal meaning to the verbal expression. Silence, when it substitutes and interrupts speech or a communicative sound, is also a paralinguistic act.

Kinesics [172] is body language, any movement from muscular or skeletal shift. These body movements result in such acts as postural expression, facial expression, and gestures. Kinesic acts also convey meaning to the interaction between human beings. These nonverbal components contribute to communication in a definable structure. They correlate with language and are themselves systems which are indispensable concomitants to communication. In fact, speech acts cannot be understood correctly or interpreted in any meaningful way without taking kinesic acts into consideration.

Male and female differences in human behavior signaling masculinity and femininity are perhaps conveyed more by nonverbal means than any other way. All people walk and talk, but females walk and talk differently from males. When we examine the paralinguistic and kinesic variables of male and female behavior, it is necessary to take into account temporal and cross-cultural differences throughout history and throughout the world. What may have been considered male behavior at one time may not be considered mas-

*"Harry, you'll just have to learn
to speak without gesticulating."*

By Jeffrey J. Monahan; copyright © 1972 by World Magazine, Inc.; reproduced by permission.

culine at a different
point in history. Some
children's games, for
example, were once
played by adults; young
people courted in this
way during the restric-
ted days of Colonial
America. Business
men participated in
parlor games during
the 1800's, and these
games have since be-
come games only for
children. [173] One
observation concerning
female behavior (and
this is probably not
confined to nonverbal
communication but ap-
plies to other cultural
behavior as well) is
that it often coincides
with children's behavior.
The high pitch and thin quality of a woman's voice may be,
very like that of a child.

Likewise, characteristics that are said to be feminine behavior in one country may not be thought of as feminine in another country. In order to correctly determine
what are feminine and masculine behavior patterns, one must
know a great deal about the norms of behavior in many situations of a particular country, or cultural group. As I have
searched for descriptions of sex differences in paralanguage
and kinesics, I have found surprisingly little that is of substance. The comments made are often subjective and im-
precise. Worse, the descriptions may reflect prejudices
and double-standards. Several years ago, a reporter cover-
ing the Oscar awards ceremony centered his article on the
women's voices and concluded that they sounded "gosh-awful."
Here, he wrote, were the ambitious women of America and
Europe, decked out in their best with their hair perfectly
coiffured:

> Yet, their voices! Holy Eliza Doolittle! What
> sounds, what nasal sawings, what boorish bleat-

ings, what toneless mumblings, what gratings of
brass on tin, what shrill squawks, what jarring
scratches, what put-on ladylike breathings assaulted
our ears. [174]

The male voices, he went on, sounded better on the whole.
It would be difficult to honestly assess male and female dif
ferences in the atmosphere of that kind of description.

Difficulties in describing male/female paralanguage go
back to terminology, subjective judgments, and lack of specific analysis regarding paralanguage itself and the interpretation of these events, which is obscured and distorted by
double-standards. If a female talks or cries into a pillow,
it's "muffled sobbing"; if a male does the same, it's "blub-
bering," with negative connotations. Added to the difficulties
created by double-standards and prejudices, are the difficulties
of being scientifically precise in describing such things as
voice quality and movement behavior. The scientific study
is in the very early stages of trying to define the discipline
and find rigorous, objective ways to describe a "rough/squaw-
ky/smooth/sweet/resonant/mellow/brassy-voice." Nevertheless, a few observations have been made that are worth noting.

Austin contributes several observations regarding male/
female paralinguistic behavior. Women use a higher than
usual pitch to indicate innocence, femininity, helplessness,
and regression. Males use an exaggerated low pitch to sig-
nal masculinity. But, Austin adds, low pitch has become
fashionable for women. Teen-age boys project toughness
with low pitch "O. K. you guys." The distinctive features of
oral/nasal sounds are also part of the paralinguistic system
even within a language that does not have contrasting nasal
vowel sounds. Nasality is a characteristic of the speech of
teen-age boys and men trying to appear tough. Paralanguage
carries a heavy load in courtship language--low and nasal
sounds from the male; high oral and giggling sounds from
the female. Only in the final stages is the voice low and
nasal with both sexes, but with wide pitch and intensity variation on the part of the female. When intoxicated, both
sexes produce nasal quality. Other distinctive features occurring in the paralinguistic systems signaling sex roles are
laryngealization and extra-aspiration or breathiness. Imitative behavior is exhibited by paralinguistic means. Derogatory imitation, Austin continues, is one of the most infuria-
ting acts of aggression one person can commit on another.
A male will imitate a female in high rapid speech, "Yes

dear, I'll be down in a minute" or the female may imitate
the male with exaggerated slow and low speech, "Aw, just
one more little drink. "

Though the information is sparse regarding other cultures of the world, it would appear that male/female behavior patterns are also differentiated by nonverbal means. The
Tzeltal women of southern Mexico speak with a very thin,
high-pitched quality. George Trager tells me that a Taos
Indian woman changes voice quality depending on whom she
is speaking with. To the husband and children she uses a
special high-pitch, nasalized, twangy quality, with an intense
pulsating beat. In Swedish, women but not men express a-
greement by articulating "ja" with air drawn in. The Mazateco whistle speech [175] is articulated almost exclusively by
men, though women understand and may respond verbally to
a flirtatious approach or to a whistled communication from a
son. And note that some females in our own society do not
whistle. "Whistling girls and crowing hens, Always come to
some bad end. " While crying is taboo for American males,
in Iran it is the men who weep. [176]

 . Among the Gros Ventre Indians who communicate by
sign language, Flannery noticed differences among . male and
female signers. The Gros Ventre also articulate the war
whoop which in their case, expresses joy and thankfulness,
in differing ways: the women "rattle the tongue" and the
men break the sound by striking the mouth rhythmically with
the palm. In a study of Castilian Spanish [177] it was noted
that only the male speakers used the creaky sounds of lar-
yngealized voicing. Note that in English females may use
this low, creaky voice in sensuous moods. Austin notes
marked linguistic and paralinguistic differences in male/fe-
male speech in Japan. The male speech is loud and low,
in Samurai movies almost a bark; female speech is soft and
high, almost a squeak.

Again, interpretation of nonverbal signals is a delicate
process. In Japan, the paralinguistic features which indicate
respect and politeness are breathiness, openness, lowered
volume, and raised level of pitch. Note that some of these,
for example, breathiness, quieter voice, and higher pitch
are female signals to the opposite sex in English. Teachers
of English in Japan point out the conflict for Japanese speakers:

> When the Japanese system is carried over into
> English, the results are not always as the Japanese

speaker would expect. In the case of women's
speech, (extreme examples of which might be the
girls who make announcements over the public address system in department stores, trains, etc.),
the English speaker's nearest equivalent is a kind
of feminine baby-talk usually associated with lack
of intelligence or private male-female relations.
On the other hand, female English speakers often
sound harsh, raucous, rude, or overly masculine
to a Japanese ear. [178]

Some cultures have developed paralinguistic "tools. "
Voice disguisers, instruments made by stretching a membrane
over a hollow, are used in secret ceremonies in Africa and
some other areas. [179] The voice of the speaker, a male,
is disguised by the buzzing membrane, and is thus used to
intimidate women and children and gain greater control and
discipline.

The falsetto voice is wrongly thought to be a prero-
gative of male articulation. Among the Gbeya people in the
Central African Republic, the speech of women is often modified by falsetto. The uses that were noted seem to have to
do with emotions and attitudes, but this is not clear yet. [180]
In the United States the use of falsetto is significantly different among some segments of the black population and the
white population. Both male and female Blacks may use falsetto in ways that are distinct from the use in Western cultures, though the occurrences are not clearly defined yet.
Falsetto occurs frequently in circumstances of great emotion,
either very happy or very angry. It occurs often in story-
telling and joking. Both male and female children use it
frequently. When black males use it, it does not necessarily
have the connotation of femininity. In Western societies falsetto is often used by men to imitate women, but not so in
all cultures. Among the Mohave, the male does not change[181]
to a falsetto, but using his normal voice, suggests the nuances of female speech.

In addition to vocal behavior and speech modification,
femininity and masculinity are expressed by body language
or movement behavior. This is the kinesics we defined at
the beginning of the chapter. Posture is a marked feature
and at times communicates things which can not be said.
One way to examine postural behavior is to observe the postural configurations in magazines and newspapers. A very
common feature that one will discover is that females very

often tilt their heads. This head gesture may convey an
attitude of coyness or submissiveness, but it is so common
that one can almost always find such a head position in any
group of women. A recent scientific study with film documented this kinesic behavior. [182] Two scholars of communicative behavior did an extensive study of the greeting behavior which took place at a large birthday party in a garden
setting. They analyzed the film by measuring, counting,
showing angles and distances. They categorized five positions
of the head during the greetings which took place: erect head,
head tilted forward, head tilted back, head cocked to one side,
and head held erect or forward. Males favored the forward
position: 27 out of 35 occurrences were by males. Females
tilted their head to one side significantly more than males:
18 out of 20 times recorded. The head-tilt seemed to be
more obvious in male-female greetings. An analysis of children's books showed that the vacuous, "pretty" mother is
shown in illustrations "in the classic servant's posture, body
slightly bent forward, hands clasped, eyes riveted on the
master of the house or the child. " [183]

Clothes have an effect on posture. The mini skirt
significantly affected the walking and sitting posture of females
in recent years. Mark Twain noticed the correlation of
clothes and sex in sitting posture in the famous passage where
Huck Finn, disguised in a girl's dress, gave himself away
when he closed his legs to catch something.

Facial expression is another aspect of kinesic behavior which has rich possibilities for communication between
human beings. It has been thought that females, who are
supposed to be more intuitive, could interpret these aspects
of communication better than males. The research in these
matters of sex differences, however, is highly contradictory
and ambiguous, with many variables obfuscating the results.
In the final analysis, researchers conclude that sex differences are not significant. All we can say is that some males
are more sensitive to these features than some females; and
some females are more sensitive than some males. There
are some differences in facial expression which do show sta-
tistical significance. In interaction, for example, women
look at each other more than do males. [184] It seems to
me, also, that in observing the behavior of couples with an
established relationship, the woman looks at her man much
more than he looks at her, at least in public appearances.

With regard to differences in the brain, it appears

that the visual area also has sex differences. It has been
shown that males are superior to females in certain visual-
spatial tasks. In the functioning of the right hemisphere of
the brain, males tend to have a greater left-visual field
superiority for dot location and dot enumeration than females
as we saw earlier in Chapter II. How much of this innate
difference is carried over into the life-style and masculine/
feminine behavior of human beings is not at all clear. For
just as in sound behavior, females have learned to use their
eyes in ways different from males. An old Spanish scholar
noted the many instances throughout the Spanish literature on
the references to the glances of women. [185] It would appear
to be an endless study!

Another important component of facial expression is
the mouth, with all its subtleties of shape and movement even
during speech. Study of the smile also shows significant differences in male and female use. When females approach
males, they smile. In fact, they smile more than males
throughout their lifetime, if they learned their lesson well--
that females are supposed to be pleasant and create a happy
home. A recent observer equates it to the servant's shuffle. [186]
Recent studies of the chimpanzee may suggest that this submissive gesture is of more than ancient standing. It is un-
canny how closely some of the gestural behavior of the chim-
panzees resembles that of human beings. In noting the submissive behavior throughout the discussions of chimpanzee
life, one is somehow reminded of the smile behavior of female to male human being. In describing the appeasement
and submission behavior of one of the low ranking chimpan-
zees, Jane Goodall noted that during such an encounter, he
would "pull back the corners of his lips and expose his teeth
in a nervous grin." [187]

Submissive and dominant behavior is also evidenced
in the manner of touching which male and female exhibit.
Henley shows that tactile behavior between the sexes is correlated with status dimensions. Tactile behavior in the au-
tistic realm is also a tension-reliever mechansim. Montagu
makes several observations on male/female differences noting that

> perhaps the most familiar [tension-reliever] in
> Western cultures being head scratching in men.
> Women do not usually behave in this manner; in-
> deed, the sexual differences in the use of the skin
> are marked. In states of perplexity men will rub

their chins with their hand, or tug at the lobes
their ears, or rub their forehead or cheeks or
of the neck. Women have very different gestur s
in such states. They will either put a finger on
their lower front teeth with the mouth slightly open
or pose a finger under the chin. Other masculine
gestures in states of perplexity are: rubbing one's
nose, placing the flexed fingers over the mouth, rubbing the side of the neck, rubbing the infraorbital part
of the face, rubbing the closed eyes, and picking the
nose. These are all masculine gestures; so is rubbing
the back of the hand or the front of the thigh, and pur-
sing of the lips. [188]

   The role of the speaker must be considered in describing the inventory of male/female nonverbal events. Silence must be observed by widows in some cultures but is
not required of the widower. Male/female nonverbal behavior
is closely involved with other dimensions of status and control. Consider for example, the patronizing and conciliating
tone of the male department store clerk to a woman asking
information, of a male physician to a female physician, or
of a male government official to a female reporter. He'd
better not talk that way to a man! The pattern is reversed
when a man becomes ill. The female nurse uses Baby Talk
even to mature males who command high executive positions
when they are on their feet! A study of Roman art shows
the ranking status depicted in sculpture and coinage. When
husband and wife are shown she is in the inferior position. [189]

   "Human sounds" have been studied by Ostwald, who
also observes sex differentiations among the uses and prohibitions.

Sexual prejudices and taboos against noise-making
by women may account for the fact of so few out-
standing female musicians. Traditionally women
are expected to be more contained and silent than
men, and their instruction in music was limited to
such lady-like instruments as lutes and harps.
Times change, of course, and during World War II
many noisy women were employed as boilermakers
or riveters. [190]

   The restrictions and prohibitions surrounding female
vocal behavior are of very long standing. Shakespeare recognized them and conveyed this through his characters: "Her
voice was ever soft, / Gentle and low; an excellent thing in

woman" (Lear, V, iii).   Recently a panel of bachelors described a "feminine" person as "a woman who does not talk
loudly. " In order to assess differences of behavior, one is
always brought back to consider innate sexual differences.
As we saw earlier, there do seem to be some sex differences
in the brains of males and females.   Because the research
is in very primitive stages, it is not clear yet how these
brain differences might affect the nonverbal communicative
behavior of male and female.   Another physiological difference
lies in the vocal cords and this results in higher pitched
voices for women.   Since pitch is relative, however, some
females speak with lower voices than some males.   Other
than pitch differences, male and female share equal possibilities of articulations for any verbal or paralinguistic communicative act as we observe them in languages of the world.

If then, the physiological differences are minimal, why
are the culturally learned differences so ubiquitous? Infants
are taught these learned differences at very early ages.   We
saw earlier that infants at the pre-speech stage of development were already responding to male/female differences in
intonation patterns.   Goldberg and Lewis studied early sex
differences of infants at six months and again at thirteen
months.   They found a high correlation between the behavior
of mother and resultant response of infant.   Their experiment
demonstrated that the sex-role behavior patterns are already
evident the first year of life.   Because of the differential
treatment of mothers to sons and daughters, they concluded
that parents can be active promulgators of sex-role behavior
through reinforcement of sex-role-appropriate responses during the first year.

In adolescent years, and thereafter, paralanguage and
kinesics become important in attracting sex partners.   Studies
on eye movement have indicated that eye communication is a
crucial matter in sex response patterns.   Pupil dilation occurs
in response to the desired sex. [191] Birdwhistell, who pio-
neered nonverbal messages of kinesic behavior in a rigorous,
scientific way, studied the "courtship dance" among American
teen-agers:

> We found it quite easy to delineate some twenty-
> four steps between the initial tactile contact between
> the young male and female and the coitional act.
> These steps and countersteps had a coercive order.
> For instance, a boy taking a girl's hand must await
> a counter-pressure on his hand before beginning the

finger intertwine. The move and countermove,
ideally, must take place before he "casually" and
tentatively puts his arm around her shoulders. And
each of these contacts should take place before the
initial kiss. However, there seems to be no clock-
able duration necessary for each of these steps.
The boy or girl is called 'slow' or 'fast' in terms
of the appropriate ordering of the steps, not in
terms of the length of time at each. Skipping steps
or reversing their order is 'fast. ' Insistence on
ignoring the prompting to move to the next step is
'slow. ' [192]

Chapter XII

MALE AND FEMALE AUTHORS

America's first poet was a woman. Anne Bradstreet
(1612-1672) was among the earliest immigrants from England
to settle in the New World. Her writings came out of a time
of mistrust and discouragement toward women who dared to
take time from their housewifely chores to pen a verse here
and there. Such a woman was considered immoral and received the contempt of her neighbors: "I am obnoxious [ob-
livious] to each carping tongue/ Who says my hand a needle
better fits...."[193] A man of London, in 1650, was so offend-
ed by his sister's writings that he wrote in a public letter,
"your printing of a Book, beyond the custom of your Sex,
doth rankly smell." [194]

Or such a woman was considered insane.[195] Margaret of Newcastle, for example, an author, was called the
"crazy Duchess," according to Virginia Woolf, who discusses
other women writers and their distracted states of mind. [196]
At the same time that Anne Bradstreet was writing, another
Anne, the wife of Governor Hopkins of Hartford, was also
writing. She received a typical judgment from Governor
Winthrop, who wrote in his journal for 1645:

> Mr. Hopkins, the governor of Hartford upon Con-
> necticut, came to Boston, and brought his wife with
> him ... who was fallen into a sad infirmity, the
> loss of her understanding and reason, which had
> been growing upon her divers years, by occasion
> of her giving herself wholly to reading and writing,
> and had written many books. Her husband, being
> very loving and tender of her, was loath to grieve
> her; but he saw his error, when it was too late.
> For if she had attended her household affairs, and
> such things as belong to women, and not gone out
> of her way and calling to meddle in such things as
> are proper for men, whose minds are stronger,
> etc., she had kept her wits, and might have improved

117

"You've been doodling again. All the other men are out hunting."

By Barney Tobey; copyright © 1973 by World Magazine, Inc.; reproduced by permission.

---

them usefully and honorably in the place God had set her. [197]

So intense have been the feelings about women writers, their own feelings as well as others', that only a small proportion have found their way to publish.   Some of those early writers who were able to overcome the paralyzing psychological barriers of this kind of repression did their publishing under a man's name.   Emily Brontë used the pseudonym "Ellis Bell" in the first edition of Wuthering Heights.   It was reviewed as though the author was male.   In printing the second edition, she used her own name, and thereafter the quality of the critical response changed.   It became known that all three of the Brontë sisters wrote and subsequently their writings were thought of as being "feminine."   Charlotte had recognized this hazard: "We did not like to declare ourselves women, because--without at that time suspecting that our mode of writing and thinking was not what is called 'feminine'--we had a vague impression that authoresses are liable to be looked on with prejudice...." [198]

Emily Dickinson fared somewhat better at the hands of critics who realized that her poetry was equal to the finest written in the United States. She was, however, known as a "poetess"--the very word implying that the "female nature lacked qualities essential to the creation of great poetry. "199 It is still true that there is "lacking an intellectual tradition which provides ways to think about" female writers.   "When the poetry fails it is feminine; when it succeeds it is universal. " 200 Lady Winchilsea, of the seventeenth century, was satirized as "a blue-stocking with an itch for scribbling. "201 How then can one truthfully judge a Jane Austen, a Virginia Woolf, a George Sand, a George Eliot, or a Simone de Beauvoir?

The father of Virginia Woolf, Leslie Stephen, whose name is not nearly as well-known as his daughter's, was a literary critic who is said to have "prized masculinity very highly and despised effeminacy. "202   He found the works of women novelists such as the Brontës and George Eliot to be seriously defective because of their failure to create believable male characters.   As one critic observed, "The corresponding failures of male writers to create plausible female characters seem to have troubled him far less. "202 Chesterton, another literary critic, in a penetrating discourse, reviewed the biased treatment given the male characters of female writers, and concluded, "The reply may be made that the women in men's novels are equally fallacious. " 203   It is said of Leslie Stephen, "The opposite of masculine is not feminine but morbid. " 204   Out of this atmosphere Virginia Woolf transcended sex. She realized that "it is fatal for any who writes to think of their sex. It is fatal to be a man or woman pure and simple; one must be woman-manly or man-womanly. "205

The inhibitions and restrictions limiting the use of language by women is well established in human societies. Ironically this limitation took a strange twist in Japan a thousand years ago. 206 Males, with their prestigious duties, were confined in their writings to the formal court language, which was Chinese. Thus, they produced the works of history, theology, science, and law. Women were able to create in the vernacular, the "women's language, " and thereby women writers brought about a brilliant age of literature, unique in the history of Japanese literature. Out of this, Lady Murasaki produced Genji Monogatari (The Tale of Genji), which has been acclaimed the greatest work of Japanese literature.   The Tale of Genji was written over a period of

years, about the year A. D. 1000. It has been likened to the
greatest works of fiction that the world has produced. The
influence which resulted from its central importance and from
its grandeur still survives. One of the scholars of Japanese
literature noted, "It is a remarkable and ... unexampled fact,
that a very large and important part of the best literature
which Japan has produced was written by women. " 207

He goes on to explain the causes for this and believes
that the most effective cause had to do with the position of
women in Japan at that time:

> The Japanese of this early period did not share the
> feeling common to most Eastern countries, that wo-
> men should be kept in subjection, and as far as
> possible, in seclusion. Feminine chieftains are
> frequently mentioned in the old histories, and sev-
> eral even of the Mikados were women.... Many
> instances might be quoted of Japanese women ex-
> ercising an influence and maintaining an indepen-
> dence of conduct quite at variance with our precon-
> ceived notions of the positon of women in the East.
> It is this which gives their literary work an air of
> freedom and originality which it would be vain to
> expect in the writings of inmates of a secluded
> harem.

It was during this time that Lady Murasaki gave the world
its first novel. This atmosphere was not to last, however.
The later Yedo period was very different:

> Chinese notions of the absolute subjection and the
> seclusion, as far as possible, of the [female] sex,
> made great progress. Women were now rarely
> heard of in public life, and disappear completely
> from the world of literature--a significant fact when
> we remember the feminine masterpieces of the
> Heian period. 208

In spite of the position restricting women in China, women
also influenced Chinese literature. Countless anonymous love
poems are traditionally attributed to women. 209

In another ironic historical accident, women began to
do more writing when the novel in Western culture was being
formed as another literary genre. 210 This new literature
was free from the presuppositions of a public accustomed to

male authorship of the historical epics and the Shakespearean
types of poetic drama.   The Brontës and Jane Austen were
free to explore and experiment and release their creative
powers to genre which was not yet denied to them.   In the
oral literature of ancient times, which was recorded only long
after it was originally created, it is much more difficult--
perhaps impossible--to establish whether the creators were
male or female.   We know that many of the Gaelic poets were
women.   One famous one was called Mary, daughter of Red
Alasdair.   Before she died, in 1674, she had been welcomed
all over the Highlands as a true sennachie (shanachie) who
captivated her people with living chronicles of the past. [211]

Almost a century ago, Samuel Butler put forth the
idea that a woman anonymously composed The Odyssey. [212]
Only in the last decade does this idea seem possible to believe.   Many historically obscure people are assumed to be
male even though not enough is known of their personal lives
to identify their sex.   We can now re-evaluate judgments
about literature written anonymously. [213]

Turning to more recent authorship, it still remains
that more males are listed in the card catalogs of libraries
than females, even though learning has become coeducational
and courageous women writers of the past removed the stigma
of being labeled insane and survived the contempt of society.
If one critically examines the "Acknowledgments" and credits
portions of many non-fiction books, I believe that some explanation can be found there.   Many husband-wife and pro-
fessor-student teams have produced books which have been
published as authored by a single author.   The Acknowledgments often read something like this: "To _____, Without
whom this book would not have been written" or "This book
is hers as much as mine."   After reading several dozens
of those, I began to wonder why the wife or female student,
who had done these "countless weeks of research" and "edited
every line" was not listed as a co-author?   One very honest
scholar, in an interview to the Los Angeles Times, noted
that his wife "should have been a writer.   But she always
thought my work was more important.   If she hadn't edited
my articles all these years, I would never have gotten anything published." [214]

While most men try to be generous in acknowledging
the help of their female research associates, wives or otherwise, there are some who are reluctant to acknowledge this
work.   In the extreme, a man may cite himself as a refer -

ence without stating the wife's name even though she was co-
author. It has also been a modest, socially accepted style
to list the female author as second author even though she
may have been the primary investigator. One book which
was written by a woman is listed in the card catalog under
the name of the man who wrote the Preface, because he put
his name first on the title page. On the other side of the
coin, it is pleasant to remember that there are people like
Will and Ariel Durant, who share their work and authorship.
It is not difficult, then, to conclude that women could and
did do keen intellectual research and are capable of writing,
but that often it was not the custom to acknowledge it publicly.
As Pygmalion pointed out, the expectations of society have
a controlling and manipulating effect on behavior. If society
expects little from females in the way of literature, paintings,
and music, is it any surprise that females produce relatively
little?

An evaluation of women's writings must be done along-
side evaluation of the response to their writings. A recent
president of the Modern Language Association noted that her
students invariably considered women writers inferior to men
writers. [215] This was verified in an experimental study to
evaluate the writings of women scholars and men scholars. [216]
Some 140 college women participated in the experiment.
Articles from professional journals were selected for the experiment and edited and put together in booklets that were
identical except for changes in the name of the author. In
one booklet an article would carry a male name, such as
John T. McKay. The same article would carry the name
Joan T. McKay in the other set. Each booklet contained
three articles by "men" and three articles by "women." The
women students read through the articles and then answered
a questionnaire that would rate the authors for writing style,
professional competence and status, and rate the articles for
value. The women students consistently found an article more
valuable and the author more competent when the article bore
a male name. The male pseudonyms won hands down! This
finding supports other studies where it is shown that not only
society, but females themselves feel themselves to be inferior. [217]

In judging written language it is inevitable that one is
more likely to enjoy writing which deals with subject matter
of one's own interests. How then, can one compare a book
about adventure and travel with a book about cooking; a book
about international diplomacy with a book about a child's grow-

ing up; a book about war with a book about human relationships? The subject matter of a woman's writing is limited
to the four walls of her experiences, as well as to her inter-
ests--"For women have sat indoors all these millions of
years...." [218] Then, again, who is to say that a book about
war is more important than a book about human relationships.
What are the important things in life? Virginia Woolf's mother wrote about crumbs in the bed of a sick person.

> Among the number of small evils which haunt ill-
> ness, the greatest, in the misery which it can cause,
> though the smallest in size, is crumbs. The origin
> of most things has been decided on, but the origin
> of crumbs in bed has never excited sufficient atten-
> tion among the scientific world, though it is a prob-
> lem which has tormented many a weary sufferer. [219]

This poignant passage goes on to describe the persistent crumb.
Apparently this was Julia Stephen's single publication. Holtby's
original and insightful comparison of Virginia Woolf's writings with those of her mother were reiterated in Annan's
study. [220]

Regarding subject matter, the double standard again
prevails. If a woman were to write about daffodils, it might
be passed by as trite. But when a Wordsworth writes of
daffodils, he is quoted for generations. Besides the content
of writings, there is the matter of the protagonist and the
characters that move through the scenes and chapters. A
prominent literary scholar commented, "If we were to judge
by Old English literature alone, we would conclude that only
queens, princesses, abbesses, a few wives, and a scattering
of mistresses comprised the female population of England at
that time." [221]

Jane Austen, in an imaginery conversation, expressed
the sentiments of a good many who found history dull:

> I read history a little as a duty; but it tells me
> nothing that does not either vex or weary me. The
> quarrels of popes and kings, with wars and pesti-
> lences in every page; the men all so good for noth-
> ing, and hardly any women at all, it is very tire-
> some.... [222]

History is a study of the powerful, and women have
had no power. This is the situation of women in all countries.

A study of two documents of medieval Russia shows a count
of 2400 persons; only 93 are female, or about four per cent. [223]
Indeed, our present writings of history have made no progress
in recognizing the presence of women. In a study of textbooks used in college history courses, it was discovered that
no book had more than two per cent of its pages about women.
Some had almost nothing. [224]

Virginia Woolf perceptively observes that though females are scarcely mentioned in history, they pervade poetry
from cover to cover.

> Imaginatively she is of the highest importance; prac-
> tically she is completely insignificant.... She
> dominates the lives of kings and conquerors in fic-
> tion; in fact she was the slave of any boy whose
> parents forced a ring upon her finger. Some of
> the most inspired words, some of the most pro-
> found thoughts in literature fall from her lips; in
> real life she could hardly read, could scarcely
> spell.... [225]

While books, plays, and movies are produced by the
hundreds with all male casts, almost nothing is written with
only female characters. Clare Booth Luce's recently re-
vived play, The Women is an exception. A review of The
Women said, "The cast is entirely women--which, oddly
enough detracts from it. You sometimes have a strange desire to see some of the men in the lives of these New York
society ladies...." It is doubtful that there has ever been
a review of an all-male book, movie, or drama that lamented
the all-male cast, wistfully wishing to know something of the
women in their lives! No, books are not written with women
as the main characters and with men mentioned marginally--
entering the scenes only as lovers.

While the above may be true, a curious paradox exists
in the matter of writing about male/female relationships.
Hundreds of books have been written about women and their
peculiarities, but almost none about men. The Kinsey report
is an exception. Why this morbid fascination with women,
who are left out of history?

The study of dialogue is a study of the relationships
between male and female, as well as a study of the skill of
male and female writers to successfully portray the dialogue
of real people. How can writers put words in the mouth of

a person of the opposite sex? D. H. Lawrence is a good
example to analyze, because he was concerned with male/
female relationships. Lawrence depicted how the gamekeeper
kept control over Lady Chatterley by code-switching, in the
way of manipulating his dialect to manipulate her. [226] In
addition to observing the way writers of literature depict what
they think is a viable conversation between male and female,
one can observe the way children's books depict male/female
dialogues. Linguistic behavior is culturally taught, as are
other expressions of behavior. [227] In surveying the dialogues
which occur in children's books, one notes a pathetic lack of
conversation with bright, adventurous females of any age.
Rarely is there a give-and-take dialogue in which a female
is shown to be capable of making a decision or in which a
female provides intelligent and useful information. The things
which girls and women say in these books too often reflect
the stereotypes of society: "Women are emotional." In one
book, in reference to a pleasurable experience, we read,
"One little girl thought they were so beautiful she began to
cry."

During a scene about fishing and baiting the hook, the
girl says, "I can't ... I don't want to touch those things."
"Of course you don't, here I'll do it for you." And then she
would have lost the pole but Johnny grabbed it in time. In
another story, the boy says, "You can't do it, Babs. You
will get scared if you do." "No I won't," said Babs. "Yes,
you will. You will get scared and cry."

The Little Miss Muffett syndrome, which depicts females as helpless, easily frightened, and dreadfully dull, occurs over and over again in the literature. If one compares
this image, which crystallizes in the formative years of child
development, with the potential of women in adulthood, it
becomes apparent that both male and female have difficulty
participating in equal sharing of dialogues at the professional
level. Males who have grown up learning dialogues such as
are in children's books today are not able to listen to a female in adult life. Males paralyze when a rare female makes
a constructive suggestion. Likewise females are trained not
to take their share, or hold their own in decision-making
interchange. There are no linguistic models in this early
literature for females to take active parts in the dialogue nor
for males to respond with dignified acceptance and a willing-
ness to listen. With such indoctrination as this, is it any
wonder then, that doctors don't permit women on the surgical
team and women scientists are excluded from projects and

from the laboratory where a female is thought to be useless
or a nuisance?

Finally, in this discussion of the language behavior of
male and female in the written language, we can consider
certain types of writings which were produced specifically for
female readers. Throughout the centuries, where women
could read, writings have been produced in dialects, styles,
or varieties of language which are directed to appeal to
women. Yiddish literature, for example, was first oriented
toward women readers, because women did not know how to
read in Hebrew. Pearl Buck observes that from the old
Chinese point of view, the novels were not worthy of serious
attention; they were "fit only for an idle moment of recrea-
tion or for women to read." 228 No reputable scholar would
admit to reading a novel, and if he wrote one, it would be
produced under an assumed name. Interestingly enough, these
Chinese novels, intended primarily for women, were written
with a candor and frankness that makes our pornographic
writings look tame in comparison. 229 Not all societies
"protect" women from flagrant sexual detail. In the United
States, "women's fiction" became an industry when women
began to be educated in great numbers. Between 1830 and
1860, sixty-four magazines for women were launched. 230

Chapter XIII

THE SILENT WOMAN: TYRANNY IN LANGUAGE

"Silence gives the proper grace to women. "
--Sophocles [231]

One might wonder why, in a book on language, there
is a chapter on silence. In a linguistic sense, patterns of
silence figure in language structures and must be dealt with
in the analysis of language. Thus, on a micro-level, silence
can be used to separate and give emphasis to different words.
On another level, silence separates different speakers, except in simultaneous speech or in interrupting behavior. This
kind of silence must be distinguished from nothingness, or
moments when nothing is happening. Silence is part of language and is as important as sound to communication and
thought. Silence means different things depending upon the
users: master/slave, teen-ager/adult, male/female.

In still another capacity, silence has a global meaning
among certain categories of human beings who illustrate an
intellectual or creative silence. I have been haunted through
the years by a question from one of my male students--a
sensitive, bright young scholar, who asked the old question,
"Why aren't there great women composers, artists, and writers?" The fact is, women have been "silent. " We have to
deal here with the paradox that women, with a reputation for
volubility, have made all-too-few extra-biological contributions
to society. I do not believe that the explanation for this phenomenon is strictly biological. There is a great deal of
evidence that the expectations of society--presented to each
of us at birth--are powerful enough by themselves, without
biological imperatives, to thrust males into often inappropriate roles of dominance, and to similarly paralyze females
into silence.

Ingmar Bergman created a complete film with the

main character speechless throughout the movie. The protagonist in Persona was an actress who reached a crisis before the plot was presented to the audience. She became
paralyzed--her vocal cords refused to play the game any longer. Her voice was stopped during a performance of Medea.
One cannot forget that the ancient drama of Medea dealt with
the role of motherhood. Bergman's actress was also a mother
--a classical archetype of talent conflicting with duty. In
the film the pleas and letters from home to her hospital bed
and convalescent retirement were focused on their needs for
her return to be wife and mother--not to return to her great
acting accomplishments!

In any discussion of silence, it must be made clear
that there are many varieties. 232 Silence is communicative
and there is the comforting, companionable silence between
people in equilibrium, which must be distinguished from the
negative disturbing silence of anger, fear, or hate. 233 Historically, women are expected not to make substantive verbal
contributions in the mixed social setting. Recall the conversation that D. H. Lawrence wrote to highlight the silence of
Lady Chatterley, reproduced in Chapter III. A woman's role
is to twitter about the weather, give opinions that are dull
and charming and brief, and respond with "Yes?" and "Really?"
during the men's dialogue. A male can use linguistic silence
to produce intellectual silence in women. Randolph Churchill,
Winston's father, had a maxim to handle women who wanted
to enter the discussions, "Gentlemen, there is only one reply
to a lady when she argues with you--silence. " 234

Ben Jonson (ca. 1572-1637) wrote a satiric comedy
called The Silent Woman. Elsewhere he noted that "Women
are but Men's Shadows. "235 Chaucer had also observed,
through the exceptional mouth of the Wife of Bath in Canter-
bury Tales, that women had not commented on men in anything
like the manner that men had written of women. Indeed, as
we noted before, a trip to any library and a browse through
the stacks will show shelf after shelf of books about women--
written by men. What do women have to say--about themselves ... or the world around them? It is a commonplace
that silence is necessary for deep thought--for either the
artist or the scientist. The centuries of women's silence
might be explained, in part, by the repression caused by not
having private periods of productive silence. Lack of silence,
in this respect, can produce silence. 236

Mourning is a specific situation where women were

assigned to absolute verbal silence in many societies. Sir
James Frazer devotes a chapter to "The Silent Widow" in
his study of comparative religions. [237] The Silent Widow
belonged to several areas of the world: the Congo, East
Africa, British Columbia (Indians), and Australia. The period of silent mourning lasted from a few days to a year, depending upon the tribe. This restriction of silence was based
on supernatural beliefs--fears concerning the spirit of the
late husband. In Australia, where the mourning period was
lengthy, there developed gesture sign languages to continue
the necessary communications. Other vocalizations were permitted when language was prohibited. Even laughing was acceptable behavior.

Religious beliefs in Western cultures also contributed
to the muting of women. St. Paul admonished women to keep
silent in the churches. Indeed, the more conservative con-
gregations took this advice very seriously, and women were
simply not allowed to verbalize in the services in any way.
Interestingly enough, in Hastings' encyclopaedic study of religion and ethics, a section on silence is included, which covers
the worshipful and devotional silence and the monastery silence, but says nothing about the imputation of silence to women. It should not be forgotten that Jesus Christ himself
did not instruct women to be silent, but rather encouraged
them to participate. Religion must come to grips with the
conflicts imposed upon women in order for religion to be
viable.

The famous linguist Edward Sapir long ago noted sex-
discrimination and rank-discrimination, and the relationship
of these two in language. [238] The balance of power is maintained by imposing tyrannies back and forth. Females may
respond to male verbal dominance by hen-pecking or by becoming inconsolably emotional. Language differences and
nonverbal behavior (which we discussed earlier), particularly
the latter, might prove to be a measure of discrimination in
evaluating relationships in society. Silence is imposed by
various "put downs." These are subtle forms of control,
sometimes covert, usually out-of-awareness and reflecting
mental states and attitudes.

The "put downs" can take many forms, some of which
we have already discussed in previous chapters. Titles are
a way of denoting inferior status and can be used to suggest
that females do not have anything of value (to a male) to say
or contribute. Labels and descriptors imply unequal status:

"girls" would not participate in an adult discussion. Labels
can also be used as "the killing abstraction. "[239] It has
been noted that the label, "Women's Liberation, " is being
manipulated to create a counterproductive movement, which
would again silence women. It is certainly a distraction
from one's career to be asked rather pointedly, "Are you a
feminist?" While language is a means of communication, it
can also be used to misdirect human beings. Flattery is a
deceptive put-down; used by a male, it can fool the listener
into thinking she is valued highly. One does not hear the
blarney poured out to experts and authoritative figures--they
don't need it. "Explanations" are very often subtle put-downs.
Observation shows that explanations usually go one way: male
to female. It is unladylike for a female to explain a concept.

Categories are another way of putting women aside.
Several examples were given in Chapter VIII. These status
groupings continue to appear. A young man from the riot-
filled Sixties defines his situation: "I have a woman, a child,
and a dog. " A well-known educator in California prides himself: "I get along all too well with small children and with
women's clubs. " A radio discussion on street loitering listed the "freaks, widows, and kooks. " A campus newspaper
reviewed a production which satirized social ills such as economics, Women's Liberation and corrupt government. A
social studies textbook wrote that "Men trekked over the
mountains with their wives, children and cattle. "

So be it. Females, classified thusly, could hardly be
in a state of mind to be anything but silent. But, if by some
stint of courage, or overflow of knowledge or experience, a
female does start to talk, the final put-down is interruption.
Two studies have been made in California recently that indicate
the high incidence of males' interrupting females, and husbands
answering for their wives. "The hypothesis is that women ...
have restricted rights of speakership which is reflected in
male speakers' overriding the constraints of conversational
ordering when engaged in conversations with females. " [240]
In another study, which focused on visibility in the interaction
of two persons, rather unexpected findings resulted: "It
looks as if males are motivated to dominate and do so largely
by interrupting and talking more, especially when the normal
cues for floor-apportionment are absent. " [241]

All of these put-downs are socially acceptable, and the
necessary aggressive behavior that would challenge and overcome the put-down is socially unacceptable on the part of wom-
en. Thus, they are forced into patterns of silence. How and

when are these patterns of behavior learned?   And how can
they be so deeply ingrained, so that even those who know
better can hardly overcome the set patterns?   One study that
focused on the variations that children learn very early in
language behavior, noted that the first is between speech and
silence.   "Very small children will frequently talk or jabber
nonsense to their own parents or siblings, but fall silent in
the presence of strangers. " [242]   We have already noted that
male/female differences start even before this.   It is not unreasonable to extrapolate and note that females learn patterns
of silence very early.

          Tyranny, however, receives its counterbalance.   In
turn, men are the victims.   In place of silence, nagging becomes a way of dealing with a situation--a way of bringing
about an equilibrium, albeit a distasteful one.   Another way
is for the female to focus on her delicacies and purities and
not permit the male to express himself emotionally or with
"rough talk" around her or the children.   George Bernard
Shaw recognized that the most tyrannical female was the most
resolute opponent of Women's Rights. [243]   Thus, both are
losers--neither man nor woman permitted full range of expression for every human emotion.   The personality is damaged and creativity is curtailed with the inhibitions imposed.
When human beings are robbed of their dignity, all humanity
is debased.

          The truth is that a slave State is always ruled by
          those who can get round the masters: that is, by
          the more cunning of the slaves themselves.   No
          fascinating woman ever wants to emancipate her
          sex: her object is to gather power into the hands
          of Man, because she knows that she can govern him.
          She is no more jealous of his nominal supremacy
          than he himself is jealous of the strength and speed
          of his horse.   The cunning & attractive slave wo-
          men disguise their strength as womanly weakness,
          their audacity as womanly timidity, their unscrup-
          ulousness as womanly innocence, their impunities
          as womanly defencelessness; simple men are duped
          by them, and subtle ones disarmed and intimidated.
          It is only the proud, straightforward women, who
          wish, not to govern, but to be free.... [244]

We have only partially answered the question of the
young man who wondered why women haven't created to the
extent that males do.   We still have much to learn about the

brain, about creativity, about environment and learned behavior, about repression, and about the marriage dynamic. Perhaps the question cannot be satisfactorily answered until it is asked by more women. Perhaps these days we are seeing a start.

Chapter XIV

LANGUAGE CHANGE AND BILINGUALISM

Language change is, nowadays, one of the best established facts of linguistic science. Language is always in a state of flux, with outside and inner pressures and tensions molding and modifying, causing new forms to be added and old forms to be deleted. One of the factors to be considered in the theory of language change is what and/or who initiates the changes? In the observations made, if male/female linguistic behavior has been considered at all, it is generally believed that women are more conservative in their language habits and "maintain the purity of the language." It is said that the speech of women is more archaic, and indeed, Cicero said that when he heard his mother-in-law speak, it was to him "as if he heard Plautus or Nævius, for it is more natural for women to keep the old language uncorrupted, as they do not hear many people's way of speaking and thus retain what they have first learnt." 245

These kinds of assumptions are based on the belief that "innovations are due to the initiative of men." There are, of course, situations where women are cloistered or kept barefoot down in the holler with little or no contact with speakers other than the immediate community. Women in those situations would not likely be innovators of change. Language change involves linguistic processes that alter sounds from one to another, for example "learnt" to "learned"; and that change words and parts of words, such as "thou gavest" becoming "you gave." Besides linguistic processes which modify language, there are sociological and historical factors which affect language. Status must be considered, particularly in the matter of women's language. When lower status is associated with a certain form-- "ain't," for example--women are less likely to use that form because they are low enough already. Jespersen gave further examples of the important part that women have played in sound change and other changes in language. He refers to the weakening of the fully trilled tongue-point /r/ in French and also notes the involvement with

133

ON CAMPUS   with Phil Frank

REPHRA/ING THE QUE/TION /MITH - WHAT OTHER
INTERNATIONAL LANGUAGE/ ARE THERE?

status change. [246]

Women experienced a different kind of status in the
forming of the United States.   There was a shortage of wom-
en in those days and this scarcity had its effect on behavior.
The traditional "Gentlemen and Ladies" became "Ladies and
Gentlemen" in an address. [247]   It was not difficult for wom-
men to impose language behavior which was thought proper
onto males who had to succumb to this numerical tyranny.

Differing roles apparently have influenced linguistic
change in the French language in recent times.   French, of
course, has masculine and feminine grammatical genders which
are obligatory to each noun in the language.   "Le docteur"
(the doctor) is masculine, along with book, lunch, and shoe.
"La sentinelle" (the guardsman) is feminine, along with lesson,
meat, and mouth.   The usual pronoun referent would be the
masculine pronoun "he" for the first group and the feminine
pronoun "she" for the second group.   However, if the doctor
is female, the pronoun referent now is "she." This is not so

in the case of the guardsman, which retains the feminine form
"elle" in grammatical concord with the feminine gender noun.[248]
Guardsmen have not changed sex throughout the centuries, but
doctors have, and this role change appears to have affected
the linguistic habits.   In an historical event of grand propor-
tions, social revolution brought change to the Russian language.   Since 1917 women have taken on jobs and positions
which were traditionally male/masculine designated, and thus
new forms and feminine referents have made their way into
the language: obsledovatel'nica ("female investigator"), syro-
varka ("female cheese-maker"), and frezerovščica ("female
milling-machine operator"). [249]

    A factor in the degree of influence male and female
have in language change is the matter of written or unwritten
language and literate or nonliterate speakers.   Some scholars
have thought that speakers who are literate tend to keep the
old forms intact, and since in many countries only the males
are given education, the male/female differences would parallel literacy and nonliteracy in the language.   Jespersen believed that this was true of the Japanese language.   In the
Cham language of Vietnam, a similar situation occurs.   A
linguistic investigator of Cham notes that women streamline
the linguistic forms perpetuated by the Cham script. [250]
She also noted that boys evidence a change in speech when
they begin to study the script and their speech becomes more
like their fathers'.   There could be other reasons, of course,
why boys would want to imitate their fathers at this point in
their lives.   Nevertheless, it appears that women's speech
may well be a preview of the Cham language of the future.
Hoenigswald, a renowned linguist, discusses universals of
linguistic change and does not credit literacy with such powers
in linguistic maintenance. [251] Before any definitive statements
can be made, we must have more data, along with careful,
extensive studies.

    It would be enlightening, in the study of language change,
to seriously consider male/female differences.   Women's
language, which might otherwise be ignored, may retain root-
words which have been lost in the general or the literary language.   This has happened in the Zulu languages.   Both Xosa
and Zulu have a special dialect called Isi-hloɔnipa, which is
restricted to women.   Literally, the term means "the language
of having shame, " the idea resulting from a superstitious belief that if a woman uses a word identical with or similar to
her husband's name or nickname, it will bring him ill-luck.
Every generation change--or change of personnel--causes the

speakers to revert to the archaic forms, thus the women maintain very old forms of the language. [252]

Language change is often related to bilingualism or
bidialectalism, in addition to the relationship to literacy.   Earlier we noted that where there is illiteracy, it is most often
the females who are illiterate.   In bilingual situations the men
are more likely to talk the lingua franca, if it is a case of
outside contacts being necessary for economic purposes.   On
the other hand, if the people belong to a market economy,
and the women do the selling, then, of course, they know the
necessary vocabulary to carry out the bargaining.   This is
a special kind of bilingualism; the various degrees and kinds
of bilingualism make it extremely difficult to measure, in the
same way that literacy/illiteracy is difficult to measure.

There is also the matter of aural and oral bilingualism.
Many females in bilingual situations can understand the other
language but cannot speak it.   This is the situation with hundreds and thousands of Spanish-speaking women in the border
states of the United States.   Their husbands go out to work
and learn a workable English, and they stay close to home,
buying at the neighborhood grocery in Spanish, and learn only
a passive, listening English.

One of the best known examples of male/female differences is found in the Caribbean area, and, as I noted in the
first chapter, was the first one reported in the seventeenth
century among the American Indian languages.   Several centuries ago, a tribe of Karina Indians (True Carib) from the
mainland, conquered an Antillean tribe or nation which spoke
an Arawakan language.   Apparently the conquerors did not
bring their women, and so the language which was used as a
means of communication was essentially Arawakan, with over-
lays of vocabulary from the Carib language of the conquerors.
A contemporary linguist, Douglas Taylor, has studied the
situation carefully, and reports the following: [253]

> ... the language of the conquerors came to be known
> as the 'men's speech,' and was learnt with diminish-
> ing success by subsequent generations of Island-
> Carib youths; while that of the conquered Arawakan-
> speaking indigenous subsisted as the 'women's speech,
> and continued to be, in fact, the mother tongue and
> first language of all.   Today, although traces of
> this linguistic apartheid may still be found among
> the Black Carib of Central America, such differences

now amount to little more than would, in English,
those between <u>endure</u> and <u>bear</u>, <u>beverage</u> and <u>drink</u>,
<u>feeble</u> and <u>weak</u>, were the members of these pairs
but synonyms belonging, respectively to the speech
of men and to that of women.

Today most of the Carib men's language has been lost, though
there are remainders and the women know them and use them
when they want to be funny or put on the appearance of being
mannish.

Another bilingual situation which is important for its
extent and dynamic continuance is the Spanish and Guaraní
bilingualism of Paraguay. The male and female variances
are different in kind from those of the Carib-Arawak situation.
A linguist who has studied the language behavior in Paraguay
relates the use of Spanish and Guaraní respectively to dimensions of solidarity and power. Interesting differences turn
up in the observations of male/female use. For example,
young men tend to use Spanish when they start to court, in
order to show respect. As the intimacy increases and solidarity increases, they switch to Guaraní, and language which
is used in familiar situations. The matter of topics also
has something to do with language choice. Between equals,
it was observed that jokes, politics, sports, and women are
discussed in Guaraní, whereas school subjects, legal matters,
and business affairs are discussed in Spanish. [254]

In a previous chapter we noted that Japanese women
were superior in the writings of the literature during the
period when Chinese was being used at court. This is a
remarkable illustration of a monolingual condition actually
being an advantage. The males, who were bilingual, were
not able to excell in their writings because of the restrictions
put upon them in writing in their own vernacular. Another
unusual situation is from Africa. The Sango language is
spoken in the Central African Republic, and a linguist who
has lived there for many years and knows the language well
reports that, "Men claim not only that the women living in
the towns speak the language better than they do but also
that the Sango of the women sounds good: <u>anzere mingi</u> 'it
is very sweet'. "[255]

In summary, we see that there are so many different
situations and so many different mixes of male/female linguistic behavior in relationship to other things that are hap-

pening in society that we must honestly admit that there is
no evidence one way or the other that either males or females
are more creative or more influential in linguistic abilities.
It is clear, however, that both males and females have the
potential for many varieties and are constantly creating new
ways to communicate across language barriers.

Chapter XV

AN ANDROGYNOUS LANGUAGE--THE FUTURE TENSE

Language Planning

In any behavioral change adjustments with resultant strains and tensions are inevitable. In some instances of behavioral change the strains are so minor one hardly notices them. In the matter of change in male and female patterns, the stakes are inestimably high and the emotions are at peak level; therefore the strains and tensions are enormous. In situations as potentially explosive as these, persons who lose their sense of humor lose themselves. Extremes of behavior will occasionally occur and there will be seemingly endless chaos. But, as in all changes of behavior, the end result will again be an orderly language system with acceptance and peaceful co-existence. Until we get to that peaceful end, we will, like our immigrant ancestors, wander between two worlds, belonging to neither one nor the other, but working toward that integrated whole which will be our permanent linguistic homeland.

Today dialogues and conversations are taking new forms. Both men and women are learning new styles and modifying linguistic forms they are no longer comfortable with. It is possible to elevate women to equal consideration and respect without putting men down. Some changes taking place today are being accepted in a relatively easy and smooth way. We have all been observing some examples. The several-volume set of reference books listing important persons in the technical world has for 65 years been known as American Men of Science. Recently the editors changed the title with little or no fan-fare, at least to the public, to American Men and Women of Science. The stylebook of the U. S. Government Printing Office now includes "Ms." in its list of acceptable titles. More and more people are using the alternatives "he or she" and "him and her" rather than the lone form "he" or "him" in their speaking and writing. The particular illustrations that I have noted are from men speakers as well as women--men who have important positions such as presiding officer, or mayors, or chancellors. Someone has suggested that the form s/he could be a useful device in the written language.   It seems worth trying.

Editors of journals are publishing revised editorial
policies advocating change that will "eliminate the subtle forms
of discrimination against women which so often are practiced
as a matter of course in the process of discussion and writing. "   The Washington Post issued a memo to the editorial
staff: "Words like divorcée, grandmother, blonde or housewife should be avoided in all stories where, if a man were
involved, the words divorcé, grandfather, blonde or house-
holder would be inapplicable. " [256]

Advertisements now include such expressions as, "The
officers and crew of S. S. _____ are men and women of gentle manners who speak your language. "   Government, business,
and school forms are being revised with terminology that includes both male and female: "this student" instead of "this
man. "   A news magazine recently substituted "Person of the
Year" for "Man of the Year. "   A newspaper account of a
recent betrothal gave equal space to the education and career
accomplishments of both bride and groom.   A 200-year-old
coeducational college is changing the last stanza of its Alma
Mater, which says, "Men may come and men may go ...
ever to thy sons a pride. "   (Incidentally, the song was written by an alumnus who had six children--all girls!)   A major
textbook company has published a "Guidelines for Improving
the Image of Women in Textbooks. " [257]

Across the nation committees are combing the textbooks
and newspapers and suggesting alternate wording such as the
following: people, human beings, or person for men/man;
telephone lineworker for lineman; seller for salesman; journalist or reporter for newspaperman; clergy for clergyman;
police officer for patrolman or policewomen; cabin attendant
for stewardess; business people for business men; members
of Congress for Congressmen; mail carrier for mailman; ordinary people for the common man/the man on the street; a
farm couple for the farmer and his wife; homeowners and
their children for a homeowner and his family; human energy
for manpower; ancestors for forefathers; the women in the
office for the office girls.

A different focus is suggested for some phrasing:
"Marie Curie did what few people could do, " for "Marie Curie
did what few people--men or women--could do. "   "Women in
ancient Egypt had considerable control over property" for
"The ancient Egyptians allowed women considerable control

over property. " 258   A news account reported, "A driver
was stalled ... " instead of "A woman stalled her car.... "
These changes are being made and suggested by both men and
women, it should be noted.   Males who are interested in fair-
ness and consideration for all persons have come out with
strong statements and guidelines. 259

The examples quoted above are all articulated quite
easily and move smoothly into speech acts without major adjustments in linguistic structures and rhythm patterns.   There
remain some difficult problems.   There will be indecision and
uncertainty until a solution is worked out for such anomalous
forms as "Madame Chairman. "   The matter of pronoun referent is still a burden.   The use of "he" alone is unsatisfactory
in view of past history leaving women out of the scene.   There
needs to be some evidence that the females are in consideration.   Suggestions for a new pronoun that does not differentiate have been made on many occasions.

In the last century a serious attempt was made to add
another form to the set of referents that would solve the he /
she dilemma.   Charles Crozat Converse, a musician and
lawyer, introduced a new word, "thon, " which he constructed
from "that one" with the idea that it would take the place of
"he" or "she. "   By 1889 it had received some attention and,
Converse claimed, had "gained the consent of many eminent
philologists. "   His efforts made enough impact for the word
to be included in the entries of Webster's second edition,
where it was glossed as "a proposed genderless pronoun of
the third person. "   Interest faded so completely, however,
that the third edition of Webster's did not include it.   Other
recent terminology has been put forth--all to no avail.   The
reasons are clearly linguistic, as I observed earlier.   These
pronouns belong to a set or class of linguistic forms which
is not easily expandable.   It is relatively easy to introduce
new nouns into the language: margarine, polyester, and
astronaut.   But classes of words such as pronouns remain
stable for hundreds of years without significant change.   It
is easier to change usage than to change the list of items being used.   Linguistic changes down through the ages have
followed linguistic patterns.

Other changes advocated have been the order of items
listed as in couplets: women and men instead of men and
women; female and male instead of male and female.   This
kind of change would also be difficult, I believe, again for

linguistic reasons. Rhythm in language is far more important
than most people realize--even linguists. These pairs are
only a small sample of dozens of pairs in English which have
been said as is for hundreds of years and will resist change
not because of chauvinism but because the rhythms of accent
and timing are familiar. Note other pairs which would also
be difficult or impossible to change: bread and butter, meat
and potatoes, milk and honey, bride and groom. A pair that
does seem amenable to switching is "boys and girls" or "girls
and boys." This pair does not seem to follow the strict ordering which the others preserve. Euphony also has a strong
influence on what things can be combined and in what order.
"Her or his" does not flow with ease as "His or her" because
of the particular combinations of sounds.

    Salutations in business letters to companies or unknown
persons is also a matter to be dealt with, although few suggestions and little experimentation have been tried. "Dear
Sirs" no longer pleases everyone. "Dear Friend" has been
offered, but somehow seems out of place to a business estab-
lishment. It would be additionally incongruous if the letter
were a reproach of some kind. "Gentlepeople" has been suggested, but I suspect with more tongue-in-cheek irony than
seriousness. "Ladies and Gentlemen" might accommodate in
formal situations where the persons are unspecified or unknown.

    Serious and responsible people can experiment in areas
that will encourage rational changes based on patterns of human behavior. Such a process may bring stablility to the
seeming chaos. Research in languages and linguistic studies
allied with male/female social behavior should be undertaken
in depth. There is much to be done yet in understanding the
universalities of gender systems in all languages of the world.
We don't even understand the gender system in English yet.
In order to analyze and construct theories there is a crucial
need for data. It would be useful, perhaps, to know more
about the anomalous use of gender systems in other languages
besides English. The matter of personification is of vital
importance to the study of human beings and their relationship
to their environment, and yet few studies have been made in
languages of the world on this aspect of animate and inanimate
relationship. And what of the languages of the world without
gender systems? How do they deal with male/female referents? The matter of selectional restrictions or grammatical
categories with regard to male/female conduct has not been
explored sufficiently.

Earlier I said that it would be useful to consider male/ female linguistic patterns in the matter of language change. Recently several linguists set forth some interesting questions to explore in an attempt to find a theory of language change. [260] These same questions would be useful to deal with the matter of language change in male/female usage.   Some general principles would take into consideration the following.   (1) What are the general constraints on immediately succeeding language states?   (2) How does one characterize transition between two stages of change?   How are the transitional dialects distinguished in terms of archaic/innovating features?   How does the transfer of features from one speaker to another take place?   (3) How are the observed changes embedded within larger linguistic structures and extralinguistic contexts?   How are the variables distinguished between linguistic structures and social structures?   (4) How does one evaluate changes in terms of their effect on both linguistic structures and performance factors?   (5) What actuates the change process? Linguistic change may involve stimuli and constraints from both the society around and from the structure of language. Considering the potential number of variables which may influence language change, is it possible to predict change, or is this a seemingly unsolvable problem which is common to all studies of social behavior?

So far all the statements made about male/female linguistic behavior that I can find are from societies with a strong male dominance pattern.   It would be worthwhile to investigate the linguistic patterns in societies which are matrilineal and/or have strong female influence in the decision making of the community.   There are matrilineal societies in India that might lend themselves to investigation of this kind.   The prospects seem tantalizing.   One such society is described:

> The point to be made clear is that it is the female principle in society, rather than the assumption of dominant roles by individual women, which is strengthened through the customary inheritance and name succession in the female line.   This is a subtle, but important, point.   It changes, among other things, the nature of the brother-sister relationship and, above all, that of parents to their daughters.   The strengthening of the female principle has such an impact on the general mentality that every facet of daily life is affected. [261]

If one has faithfully observed and analyzed the language of the past few years, it is patently obvious that "change is here and here to stay." It is not however altogether clear in all instances which changes will be permanent and which are yet to come. The problems for education and career choice are implicit. Parents and teachers are relating to new forms and new dialogues which they never had to deal with on the basis of sex before. Child training in the future will be directed toward developing an androgynous nature rather than diminishing or deleting certain human character-istics. The matter of performance in certain careers, such as radio broadcasting, business conferences, and political meetings is affected by male and female differences in lan-guage. Women will learn to produce authoritative intonation patterns in speech in addition to passive listening cooings. Women will learn not to be so "sweet" and dainty and help-less in their voices, as they assume responsibilities that all adults must assume to keep a society running smoothly and pleasurably for all. Men will have to learn, as women have been doing for thousands of years, to stay in there and con-tinue the conversation even after a put-down. Men are going to learn to respond to the command form, "Bring me an ash-tray!"

"The time has come when men must care--if not for woman's sake, for man's," said Clare Boothe Luce. [262] Men's relationships to society in terms of power and compe-tition must be examined and modified. D. H. Lawrence ob-served that "there are two kinds of power: the power to dominate others, and the power to fulfill oneself." Lawrence wrote that "The leader-cum-follower relationship is a bore.... And the new relationship will be some sort of tenderness, sen-sitive, between men and men, and between men and women."[263]

I would suggest that perhaps the most urgent problem of human beings, if the ecologist and the peace-maker will bear with me, is the friendship of male and female. Personal satisfaction and fulfillment might preclude the "need" to wage war and contaminate the environment. Overpopulation and war are results of more profound problems. If the male/female relationships were satisfying to begin with, we would not have the need to try to "fulfill" ourselves with distracting activities. Robert Graves wrote, "The most important his-torical study of all, utterly dwarfing all economic and political ones, is for me the changing relationship between men and women down the centuries...."[264] Too often and for too long it has been the central theme that any relationship between

male and female peers is only a sexual relationship. As
someone has said, "The friendship of a man and woman is
one of the most unexplored of all human experiences.... "[265]
Unexplored it is, but not exactly new. Another scholar of a
former generation noted both that "the love (sex) relationship
between men and women is only one of the many kinds of relationships possible and desirable, and that they must learn
to accept each other primarily as human beings, and only
secondarily as beings of different sex. " [266] This brings us
back to the line drawing in the first chapter where we considered whether human/nonhuman or male/female had the
higher priority. If the conceptual treatment of human beings
moves toward the human having the higher hierarchy, then
the language will likewise assume those shapes.

      Such a language can be called an androgynous language.
The contemporary ideas revolving around androgyny seem to
go back, in recent times, at least, to Coleridge's remark:
"The truth is, a great mind must be androgynous. " [267] As
we saw earlier, the mind of the Aztec and the Chinese probably had a realistic comprehension of the dual nature of human
beings--or the androgynous nature. It is not unlikely that
their language structure aided them in not distorting the balance between male and female principles. The Indo-European
languages, with their obligatory sex and gender markings, make
it more difficult to grasp qualities in the human being without
their being relegated to a male or a female division. It is
probable that in the origin of human beings, neither sex was
more important, nor more dominant. In order to survive,
both had to be equally important, in their own ways. In the
development of civilizations, an imbalance gradually took over,
and progressed with increasing ferocity, until the time when
people began to talk of the Battle of the Sexes.

      Now, with the inventions of destruction readily avail-
able to anyone, it is time to return to the androgyny that
precludes sexual competition and anticipates cooperation. Life
is difficult enough as it is. Though the linguistic examples
in this book make it appear the language problem is worse for
females, this is not the whole picture. Men's lives have been
shortened by burdens too great for them to bear alone. The
perpetual struggle has been harder on men than on women
who have received their benefits and pensions, and now "enjoy"
them alone.

      Virginia Woolf developed the androgynous concepts more
fully than any other writer up until her time. Beginning with

Coleridge's idea, she worked toward the fusion in the mind
that would evoke all its faculties--"... a mind that is purely
masculine cannot create, any more than a mind that is purely
feminine. "

> ... the androgynous mind is resonant and porous; ...
> it transmits emotion without impediment; ... it is
> naturally creative, incandescent and undivided. In
> fact one goes back to Shakespeare's mind as the
> type of the androgynous, of the man-womanly mind
> .... And if it be true that it is one of the tokens
> of the fully developed mind that it does not think
> specially or separately of sex, how much harder it
> is to attain that condition now than ever before. [268]

Shakespeare may have been the greatest androgynous
writer, but he was by no means the only one. Critics will
go back now, and rediscover many other writers who wrote
neither as male nor female. It is interesting to note that an
early review of Jane Eyre observed that it had the mark of
both a male and a female mind. [269] George Bernard Shaw
is another keen observer that people will reexamine now as
they realize his androgynous attitudes. He explained that the
secret of his extraordinary knowledge of women was due to
his assuming that they were persons exactly like himself. [270]
He recognized the conflict in women for what it was:

> Social questions are produced by the conflict of hu-
> man institutions with human feeling. For instance,
> we have certain institutions regulating the lives of
> women. To the women whose feelings are entirely
> in harmony with these institutions there is no Woman
> Question. But during the present century, from the
> time of Mary Wollstonecraft onwards, women have
> been developing feelings, and consequently opinions,
> which clash with these institutions. The institutions
> assumed that it was natural to a woman to allow
> her husband to own her property and person, and
> to represent her in politics as a father represents
> his infant child. The moment that seemed no longer
> natural to some women, it became grievously oppres-
> sive to them. Immediately there was a Woman
> Question, which has produced Married Women's Prop-
> erty Acts, Divorce Acts, Woman's Suffrage in local
> elections, and the curious deadlock to which the
> Weldon and Jackson cases have led our courts in the
> matter of conjugal rights. When we have achieved

reforms enough to bring our institutions as far into
harmony with the feelings of women as they now are
with the feelings of men, there will no longer be a
Woman Question.   No conflict, no question. 271

To live an androgynous life, one must have an androgynous language.   Both males and females will work toward
such a dynamic language that will exhibit neither chauvinsim
nor bitter grievances.   The "new" language will be concerned
with quality of life rather than power.   People will work toward achieving a style that is a personal style--neither masculine nor feminine.   Women should not try to copy the language of the male, even though it has been the language of
politics and history.   She should not try to speak "like" men,
nor to think "like" men.   This would only replace one inadequate model for another.   Women will never be freed by imi-
tating masculine behavior.   Shaw insightfully commented: "It
was clear to me that what women had to do was not to repu-
diate their femininity, but to assert its social value; not to
ape masculinity, but to demonstrate its insufficiency. " 272

An androgynous language will be complementary rather
than divisive.   It will find balance and harmony in its com-
pleteness.   It will establish an equilibrium in its unity rather
than invidious separation.   It will combine the abstract with
the concrete;   feeling with logic, tenderness with strength;
force with graciousness.   It will be a balanced tension--sup-
porting rather than opposing.   It will be exuberant and vibrant,
leaving out the weak and the brutal.   It will not tolerate the
simpering, helpless, bitchy sweetness of the "feminine" language.   Nor will it tolerate the overwhelming smash of the
opinionated and blustering "masculine" language.   It will move
away from the cruel distinctions that have wounded both male
and female human beings.

In the days when an androgynous language is spoken,
women will be freed from the repression that has resulted
in hesitant language or silence.   Men will be freed to creativity when they can permit themselves sensitivity and intui-
tion.   Men will profit from passiveness when it implies an
emptiness and receptiveness that is able to receive a new
thought--a creation--an idea born in its time--an invention
that will produce.   The androgynous life will be the next important evolutionary development, for the Act of Creation will
not be complete until male and female become a balanced
event.

CHAPTER NOTES*

CHAPTER I

1. De Beauvoir, p. 74. There is some doubt among classical scholars that Pythagoras wrote anything. Nevertheless, even if this quotation is not actually his, it reflects the philosophical environment of the times, and the theory of opposites in dualistic form was prevalent in his school of thinking. "There was a theoretical distinction between male and female per se: in the Table of Opposites, Female stands on the left side along with Darkness, Evil, the Unlimited and the rest" (Kathleen Freeman, The Pre-Socratic Philosophers, Oxford: Basil Blackwell, 1966, pp. 82-83). Before condemning Pythagoras too highly, though, it should also be remembered that Pythagoras addressed himself to women as well as to men, and women were among the first to enter his school.
2. Newsweek, December 6, 1971, p. 58.
3. Robin Morgan, Monster, New York: Random House, 1972.
4. The examples in this paragraph arc from Jespersen, 1921, pp. 243-253.
5. Encyclopaedia Britannica, Vol. 23, "Women," p. 705.
6. Lasch, p. 96.
7. R. Priebsch, and W. E. Collinson, The German Language, [1934] rev. 5th ed., New York: Barnes and Noble, 1962, p. 293.
8. Otto Weininger, Sex and character, New York: G. P. Putnam's Sons, 1906, p. 189. On the other hand, "Woman is soul," de Beauvoir, p. 167.
9. Barbara Bellow Watson, A Shavian guide to the intelligent woman, New York: W. W. Norton, 1964, p. 17.

---

* Complete bibliographical data for works that are of primary interest to male/female language, and which are in these notes cited by author's last name only, are found in the Bibliography, which follows the Chapter Notes. Other references and works of peripheral interest are cited in full here.

10. Jespersen, 1921, p. 253.
11. Inge K. Broverman, et al., "Sex-role stereotypes and clinical jugments of mental health," Journal of Consulting and Clinical Psychology, 34:1 (1970), pp. 1-7.
12. Mary Jane Sherfey, "The evolution and nature of female sexuality in relation to psychoanalytic theory," Journal of American Psychoanalytic Association, 14:1 (1966), pp. 121-122. (Parts of this article were reprinted in Robin Morgan, ed., Sisterhood is powerful, New York: Random House, 1970, pp. 220-230.) John Money, "Psychosexual differentiation," in Sex research: new developments, New York: Holt, Rinehart and Winston, 1965, p. 8. See also de Beauvoir, Chapter I.
13. With apologies to John Ciardi, World, May 22, 1973, p. 8, who, I hope, is still my friend after nullifying his beautiful palindrome.
14. Stanley.
15. J. C. Catford, "The articulatory possibilities of man," in B. Malmberg, ed., Manual of Phonetics, Amsterdam: North-Holland Pub. Co., 1968, p. 310.
16. Uhlenbeck's review, p. 94.
17. Robert Graves, Man does, woman is, New York: Doubleday, 1964. The idea was earlier articulated by de Beauvoir, p. 336.
18. See Roman Jakobson, "Linguistics," in Main trends of research in the social and human sciences, The Hague: Mouton, pp. 426-431, for other discussion and references on economics and linguistics.
19. R. M. Glasse and M. J. Meggitt, eds. Pigs, pearlshells and women: marriage in the New Guinea Highlands, Englewood Cliffs, N.J.: Prentice-Hall, 1969.
20. Graves, 1965, p. 108.
21. See Watson (note 9), pp. 105-108.
22. Mary Ritchie Key, "A language-category test: from a composite culture," duplicated by Orange County Department of Education, Spring 1971.
23. Daniel Brinton, Arawak of Guiana, Philadelphia, 1871.
24. Harold Key and Mary Ritchie Key, Vocabulario Mejicano [Aztec] de la Sierra de Zacapoaxtla, Puebla, Mexico, D. F., 1953.
25. For this discussion I have drawn heavily from the distinguished Mexican scholar, Miguel León-Portilla, Aztec thought and culture: a study of the ancient Nahuatl mind, Norman: University of Oklahoma Press, 1963; and "Philosophy in the cultures of ancient

Mexico, " in F. S. C. Northrop and Helen H. Liv-
ingston, eds. , Cross-cultural understanding: epis-
temology in anthropology, New York: Harper and
Row, 1964, pp. 35-54. (León-Portilla is not to
be blamed for my interpretation!) Also see Alfonso
Caso, The Aztecs, Norman: University of Oklahoma
Press, 1958; Jacques Soustelle, The daily life of
the Aztecs, Penguin Books [1955] 1961; and George
C. Vaillant, The Aztecs of Mexico, rev. by Susannah
B. Vaillant, New York: Doubleday, 1962.

26. León-Portilla, 1963, p. 90, from note 25.

CHAPTER II

27. Jane van Lawick-Goodall, In the shadow of man. Boston:
Houghton Mifflin, 1971.
28. Gail Shea, "Sex role sociolization, " in 51% Minority,
Connecticut Conference on the Status of Women,
National Education Association, USOE-0-72-2507,
1972, pp. 28-30.
29. John Money, "Psychosexual differentiation, " in Sex research: new developments, ed. by John Money,
New York: Holt, Rinehart and Winston, 1965, p. 12.
30. Doreen Kimura, "The asymmetry of the human brain, "
Scientific American, March 1973, pp. 70-78.
31. Edward T. Hall, The silent language, New York: Doubleday, 1959, p. 49.
32. Diana Scully, and Pauline Bart, "A funny thing happened
on the way to the orifice: women in gynecology
textbooks, " American Journal of Sociology, 78:4
(January 1973), p. 1048.
33. Gerald Holton, "Presupposition in the construction of
theories, " in Edward M. Jennings, ed. , Science
and literature, Anchor Books, 1970, p. 252.
34. Weston LaBarre, The human animal, 1954, pp. 276-277.
35. Graves, 1965, p. 50. Deborah and Barak are characters
from the Old Testament (Judges 4 and 5). Deborah
was a great judge of Israel, who ruled with remarkable intuitive wisdom. She commanded Barak to
go against Sisera, the commander-in-chief of Jabin's
army with 900 iron chariots. Barak only agreed
to go if she would go with him. Together they won
the battle and afterwards sang together in triumph.
Graves says that:
No release from the present impasse can come,
in my view, except from a Barak who has
put himself under Deborah's orders. Barak

means 'lightning', but is associated with
báraka, or 'blessedness' that comes from
divine Wisdom. Potential Deborahs are
not uncommon even today, but the Jabins
and Siseras make every effort to limit their
activities and sap their self-reliance. The
Deborahs either resign themselves to marriage, or commit some spectacular form
of suicide, or are confined to the psychotic
wards of mental hospitals. It is the Baraks
who are missing from the scene, or who
fail to answer their summons. "

36. Richard Wilhelm, The I Ching; or, Book of changes,
      Princeton, N;J. : Princeton University Press, 1967
      (Bollinger series XIX). For further discussion of
      the duality of non-Western thought, see de Beauvoir,
      p. xvi.

CHAPTER III

37. Philipp Wegener, Untersuchungen uber die Grundfragen
      des Sprachlebens, 1885. I expand on his ideas in
      "Nonverbal behavior in speech acts, " paper read
      at the conference, "Sociology of language and theory
      of speech acts, " Bielefeld, Germany, April 1973.
      This material is included in my book on nonverbal
      communication, "The context of situation in a theory
      of communication, " Paralanguage and kinesics,
      Chapter VII, Metuchen, N. J. : Scarecrow Press,
      1975.

38. See the Aztec dictionary, Vocabulario Mejicano, by
      Harold Key and Mary Ritchie de Key (Mexico, D.
      F. : 1953) for definitions.

39. The Aztec example was taken from Erich Neumann, The
      Great Mother, Princeton, N. J. : Princeton University
      Press, 1955, pp. 200-202.

40. I am grateful to Harold Key for this exposition. I have
      consulted with several Aztec scholars about this
      word and they are in general agreement that the
      interpretation was misused. See also Miguel León-
      Portilla's, Aztec thought and culture, Jacques
      Soustelle's, The daily life of the Aztecs, and George
      C. Vaillant's, Aztecs of Mexico (for all three works,
      see note 25).

41. Cratis D. Williams, "Metaphor in mountain speech, "
      Mountain Life and Word, 38:4 (Winter 1962), pp. 9-12

42. Eric Partridge, Swift's polite conversation: with intro-
      duction, notes and extensive commentary, New York:
      Oxford University Press, 1963, pp. 13-14, 28.
43. D. H. Lawrence, Lady Chatterley's lover, New York:
      Grove Press, 1957, pp. 72, 77-78.
44. Charles A. Ferguson, "Baby talk in six languages,"
      The ethnography of communication, American An-
      thropologist, 66:6 (December 1964), pp. 103-114.

CHAPTER IV

45. Dorothy L. Sayers, "The human-not-quite-human," in
      Unpopular opinions: twenty-one essays, New York:
      Harcourt, Brace, 1947, p. 148.
46. Simeon Potter, "Etymology and meaning," Chapter 9,
      Our language, Penguin Books, 1959, p. 106.
47. De Beauvoir, pp. xvi, 167.
48. Ellis and Abarbanel.
49. Wilfred Funk, Word origins and their romantic stories,
      New York: Grosset and Dunlap, 1950, p. 247.
50. Wayland F. Dunaway, The Scotch-Irish of Colonial Penn-
      sylvania, Chapel Hill: University of North Carolina
      Press, 1944, p. 132.

CHAPTER V

51. See for example, such articles as: Roger Brown and
      Marguerite Ford, "Address in American English,"
      Journal of Abnormal and Social Psychology, 62:2
      (1961), pp. 375-385; and Dan I. Slobin, Stephen H.
      Miller, and Lyman W. Porter, "Forms of address
      and social relations in a business organization,"
      Journal of Personality and Social Psychology, 8:3
      (1968), pp. 289-293.
52. See Goldberg.
53. Donald Dean Parker, Scottish and Scotch-Irish ancestry
      research, (mimeo. ed.) Santa Fe, N.M.: n.p., n.d.,
      p. G. 5.
54. Rosalie Fellows Bailey, "Dutch systems in family nam-
      ing: New York--New Jersey," Genealogical Publica-
      tions of the National Genealogical Society, No. 12
      (1954), p. 12.
55. Elvira M. Townsend, revised by Mary Key, "Names
      and titles," Latin American courtesy, Summer
      Institute of Linguistics, 1961, pp. 25-27.

154   Male/Female Language

56. Mead, 1949, p. 266.
57. According to the Gallup Poll, Los Angeles Times, March 12, 1973.
58. Atwood.
59. Zoltán Bánhidi et al., Learn Hungarian, Budapest, 1965, p. 52.
60. Ambrose Bierce, The enlarged devil's dictionary, New York: Doubleday, 1967, p. 197.
61. Los Angeles Times, June 4, 1972.

CHAPTER VI

62. Jespersen, 1921, p. 239.
63. Vance Rudolph, "Verbal modesty in the Ozarks," Dialect Notes, 6 (1928-1939), American Dialect Society, p. 57.
64. Lynne S. Crumrine, "An ethnography of Mayo speaking," Anthropological Linguistics, 10:2 (February 1968), pp. 19-31.
65. Robert Murphy, "Social structure and sex antagonism," Southwestern Journal of Anthropology, 15 (1959), p. 92.
66. For other examples, see Robin Morgan, Sisterhood is powerful, New York: Random House, 1970, pp. 526-527.

CHAPTER VII

67. Lester Warren Sontag and Robert F. Wallace, "The movement response of the human fetus to sound stimuli," Child Development, 6 (1935), pp. 253-258.
68. Margaret Bullowa, "The start of the language process," Actes de Xe Congrès International des Linguistes, Bucarest, 1967. Editions de l'Academie de la République Socialiste de Roumanie, 1970, pp. 191-200.
69. T. Berry Brazelton, and Grace C. Young, "An example of imitative behavior in a nine-week-old infant," Journal of the American Academy of Child Psychiatry, 3:1 (January 1964), pp. 53-67.
70. Biological rhythms in psychiatry and medicine, Publication No. 2088, Washington, D. C.: U. S. Government Printing Office, 1970, pp. 4, 36-38. See also William S. Condon and Louis W. Sander, "Neonate movement is synchronized with adult speech:

interactional participation and language acquistion, "
Science 183 (January 11, 1974) pp. 99-101.

71. Peter H. Wolff, "The natural history of crying and other
vocalizations in early infancy, " in B. M. Foss,
ed. , Determinants of infant behavior IV, London:
Methuen, 1969, pp. 81-109.

72. Ruth H. Weir, "Some questions on the child's learning
of phonology, " in Frank Smith and George A. Miller,
eds. , The genesis of languages, Cambridge, Mass. :
MIT Press, 1966, p. 156.

73. Philip Lieberman, Intonation, perception, and language.
Cambridge, Mass. : MIT Press, 1968, p. 45.

74. References for several studies reflected in these para-
graphs are found in Lewis.

75. O. C. Irwin, "Phonetical description of speech development in childhood, " in L. Kaiser, ed. , Manual of
Phonetics, Amsterdam: North-Holland Pub. Co. ,
1957, pp. 403-425.   Sister Helen Daniel Malone,
"An analysis and evaluation of. phonemic differences
in the speech of boys and girls at the kindergarten,
first, second and third grade levels, " Dissertation,
University of Michigan, 1954, microfilms A 54-1871.

76. Paula Menyuk, Sentences children use, Cambridge, Mass. :
MIT Press, 1969, p. 19.   Mildred C. Templin,
"The study of articulation and language development
during the early school years, " in Frank Smith and
George A. Miller, eds. , The genesis of language,
Cambridge, Mass. : MIT Press, 1966, pp. 173-186.

77. Jean Berko, "The child's learning of English morphology,"
Word, 14 (1958) pp. 150-178. (Reprinted in Sol
Saporta, ed. , Psycholinguistics, New York: Holt,
Rinehart and Winston, 1961, pp. 359-375.)

78. Gleason.

79. Norma Farquhar, Susan Dunn, and Elizabeth Burr, "Sex
stereotypes in elementary and secondary education, "
Westside Women's Committee, Los Angeles, 1972.

80. Schuell.

81. Mildred Dawson and Georgiana Collis Newman, Language
teaching in kindergarten and the early primary
grades, New York: Harcourt, Brace and World,
1966, pp. 3-4.

82. Eleanor E. Maccoby, The development of sex differences,
Palo Alto, Calif. : Stanford University Press, 1966,
p. 26.

83. Patricia Sexton, "How the American boy is feminized, "
Psychology Today, 3:8 (January 1970), pp. 23-29,
66-67.

84. Edward T. Hall, The silent language, New York: Double-
    day, 1959, p. 120.
85. Stanchfield, n. d.
86. Stevenson Smith, "Age and sex differences in children's
    opinion concerning sex differences," Journal of Ge-
    netic Psychology, 54 (1939), p. 20.
87. Mirra Komarovsky, "Cultural contradictions and sex
    roles," American Journal of Sociology, 52:3 (No-
    vember 1946), p. 187.   Reprinted in Judith M.
    Bardwick, Readings on the psychology of women,
    New York: Harper and Row, 1972.
88. Hugh Sykes Davies, "Grammar and style," in Paul C.
    Wermuth, Modern essays on writing and style, New
    York: Holt, Rinehart and Winston, 1964, p. 19.
89. Kagan, especially pp. 156-163.
90. Richard L. Tobin, "Illiteracy, woman's worldwide bur-
    den," Saturday Review, September 5, 1970, p. 16.

CHAPTER VIII

91. Ideas for this chapter were first presented at the annual
    meeting of the American Dialect Society, New York,
    December 1970.   A slightly revised version of the
    paper was later published: Mary Ritchie Key, "Lin-
    guistic behavior of male and female," Linguistics:
    An International Review, 88 (August 1972), pp. 15-
    31.   Most of it is included with the permission of
    the publisher, in chapters VIII and IX.   There are
    some revisions.
92. Complete references for the following examples are
    found in the bibliography.   For linguistic rules that
    govern these examples see the articles: for Cham,
    Blood, pp. 140-141; for Gros Ventre, Flannery, p.
    134; for Koasati, Haas, p. 143; for Yana, Sapir,
    1929, p. 208.
93. Suniti Kumar Chatterji, "Bengali Phonetics," Bulletin
    of the School of Oriental Studies, 2 (Pt I), London,
    (1921), p. 6.
94. Fischer.
95. Ralph W. Fasold, "A sociolinguistic study of the pro-
    nunciation of three vowels in Detroit speech," Wash-
    ington, D. C.: Center for Applied Linguistics, mimeo,
    1968.
96. Lewis Levine, and Harry J. Crockett, Jr., "Speech
    variation in a Piedmont community: postvocalic r,"
    International Journal of American Linguistics, 33:4

(Pt. II), (1967), pp. 76-98. See also Shuy.

97. Elizabeth Uldall, "Dimensions of meaning in intonation, " in David Abercrombie, et al., In honour of Daniel Jones, London: Longmans, 1964, p. 274.

98. Brend.

99. Ben Graf Henneke, and Edward S. Dumit, The announcer's handbook, New York: Holt, Rinehart and Winston, 1959, p. 19.

100. Ekka, pp. 26-27.

101. Norma Faust.

102. Meredith, 1930, p. 476.

103. Dwight Bolinger, Aspects of language. New York: Harcourt, Brace and World, 1968, p. 112. See also Charles Barber, Linguistic change in present-day English. University of Alabama Press, 1964, pp. 105-106.

104. Greene, p. 14.

105. Wise.

106. Erades, p. 5.

107. Jespersen, 1921, p. 250.

108. I would particularly like to mention the extensive research project of Deanna Deeley Spehn.

109. Jo Freeman, "The building of the gilded cage, " duplicated, KNOW, 16 pp. and Edward M. Bennet and Larry R. Cohne, "Men and women: personality patterns and contrasts, " Genetic Psychology Monographs 59 (1959), pp. 101-155.

110. Lakoff, pp. 53 ff.

111. E. A. Levenston, "Imperative structures in English, " Linguistics 50 (July 1969), pp. 38-43.

112. Ben G. Blount, "Parental speech and language acquisition: some Luo and Samoan examples, " Anthropogical Linguists, 14:4 (April 1972), p. 130.

113. Carolyn G. Heilbrun, Toward a recognition of androgyny, New York: Knopf, 1973, p. 161.

114. Jespersen, 1924, pp. 55-57.

115. Benjamin Lee Whorf [ca. 1937], "Grammatical categories," Language, 21:1 (1945). Reprinted in John B. Carroll, ed., Language, thought, and reality: selected writings of Benjamin Lee Whorf, Cambridge, Mass.: MIT Press; New York: John Wiley, 1962, pp. 87-10 101.

116. Jerrold J. Katz and Jerry A. Fodor, "The structure of a semantic theory, " Language, 39 (1963), pp. 170-210. Reprinted in Jerry A. Fodor and Jerrold J. Katz, eds., The structure of language: readings in the philosophy of language, Englewood Cliffs, N. J.:

Prentice-Hall, 1964, especially p. 517.
117. Material for this discussion is found in the following
     references: D. Terence Langendoen, The study
     of syntax, New York: Holt, Rinehart and Winston,
     1969, p. 37. James D. McCawley, "The role of
     semantics in a grammar, " in Emmon Bach and
     Robert T. Harms, eds., Universals in linguistic
     theory, New York: Holt, Rinehart and Winston,
     1968, pp. 140, 134. Paul M. Postal, "On so-
     called 'pronouns' in English, " Monograph on Lan-
     guages and Linguistics No. 19, Washington, D. C. :
     Georgetown University Press, 1966, reprinted in
     David A. Reibel and Sanford A. Schane, eds. ,
     Modern studies in English, Englewood Cliffs, N. J. :
     Prentice-Hall, 1969, p. 208. Roderick A. Jacobs,
     and Peter S. Rosenbaum, English transformational
     grammar, Waltham, Mass. : Blaisdell Pub. Co. ,
     1968, p. 63. Mansoor Alyeshmerni, and Paul
     Taubr, Working with aspects of language [workbook],
     New York: Harcourt, Brace and World, 1970, p.
     184. Jeffrey Gruber, "Functions of the lexicon in
     formal descriptive grammar, " Santa Monica: Sys-
     tem Development Corporation, TM 3770/000/00,
     1967, pp. 37, 24.
118. The last two examples are from Eli Ginzberg, Life
     styles of educated women, New York: Columbia
     University Press, 1966.
119. Jerome S. Bruner, et al. , A study of thinking, New
     York: John Wiley, 1956, pp. 7, 267.
120. Franz Boas, "On grammatical categories, " Handbook
     of American Indian languages, reprinted in Dell
     Hymes, ed. , Language in culture and society, 1964.
     Benjamin Lee Whorf, "Grammatical categories, "
     Language, thought, and reality, 1956. Edward
     Sapir and Morris Swadesh, "American Indian gram-
     matical categories, " reprinted in Hymes, 1964.
121. Francis P. Dinneen, An introduction to general linguis-
     tics, New York: Holt, Rinehart and Winston, 1967,
     pp. 152-153.
122. Samuel E. Martin, in Hymes, pp. 407-415.

                        CHAPTER IX

123. Whorf, pp. 91-92.
124. Jespersen, 1933, p. 190.
125. The following two examples are taken from Sutton, p. 8.

126. John B. Carroll, Peter Davies, and Barry Richman,
        eds., The American Heritage word frequency
        book, Boston: Houghton Mifflin, 1971.
127. Key, 1971, p. 172.   See the bibliography for other
        studies done on children's books.
128. Harry H. Johnston, A comparative study of the Bantu
        and Semi-Bantu languages, London: Oxford Uni-
        versity Press, 1922, p. 230.
129. Sophie C. Hadida, Manners for Millions, New York:
        Doubleday, Doran, 1933, p. 94.
130. The Roberts English series: a linguistic program, Book
        3, New York: Harcourt, Brace and World, 1966,
        p. 155.
131. For many enlightening examples, see Webster's third
        new international dictionary, Springfield, Mass.:
        G. and C. Merriam, 1966, and Louise Pound,
        "Extensions of usage of a pronoun," in Selected
        writings of Louise Pound, Lincoln: University of
        Nebraska Press, 1949, pp. 324-325.
132. William A. Stewart, "On the use of Negro dialect in
        the teaching of reading," in Joan C. Baratz, and
        Roger W. Shuy, Teaching black children to read,
        Washington, D.C.: Center for Applied Linguistics,
        1969, pp. 156-219.   See also Svartengren, 1928-
        1939, p. 48.
133. Ashok R. Kelkar, "Marathi baby talk," Word, 20:1
        (1964), p. 47.
134. Charles A. Ferguson, "Baby talk in six languages,"
        American Anthropologist, 66:6 (Pt 2), (December
        1964), pp. 106-109.
135. Jakobson, p. 541.
136. Rothstein.
137. Michalsen and Štech, p. 187; Vachek, p. 192.
138. Svartengren, 1928-1939, p. 49.
139. C. R. MacKinnon of Dunakin, The Highlands in history,
        Glasgow: Collins, 1961, p. 58.
140. Kate Millett, Sexual politics, New York: Doubleday,
        1970, p. 316.
141. See also examples in Erades, p. 3.
142. Jespersen, 1924, p. 230.
143. For some penetrating ideas, see de Beauvoir, pp. xvi,
        167.
144. Jespersen, 1924, p. 236.   Roman Jakobson, "On lin-
        guistic aspects of translation," in Reuben A.
        Brower, ed., On translation, New York: Oxford
        University Press, 1966, pp. 232-239.
145. L. S. Vygotsky, Thought and language [1934], Cambridge,

Mass. : MIT Press, 1962, p. 128.
146. Harold Whitehall, Structural essentials of English, New
     York: Harcourt, Brace and World, 1956, p. 110.
147. Svartengren.
148. Stene and Langenfelt.
149. Key, 1971.
150. See, for example, Erades, Michalsen and Štech, Svart-
     engren, and Vachek.
151. For an excellent discussion on this poem and "Sex and
     the humanization of modern life, " see Barry A.
     Marks, e. e. cummings, New Haven, Conn. :
     College and University Press, 1964, pp. 72-75.
152. Rothstein.
153. Don and Alleen Nilsen.

CHAPTER X

154. Letters, Sept. 20, 1748, ed. John Bradshaw, London:
     Allen and Unwin [1892; repr. 1926], V. 1, p. 149.
155. Fischer, p. 484.
156. L. W. Lanham, "English in South Africa, " University
     of the Witwatersrand, Johannesburg, Institute
     for the Study of Man in Africa, 1963, p. 35.
157. Trudgill, p. 180.
158. Steadman.
159. Abstract by Louisa Stark, of J. M. Lope Blanch, "La
     -r final del español mexicano y el sustrato
     nahua, " in International Journal of American
     Linguistics, 36:1 (January 1970), p. 54.
160. Robert A. Hall, Jr. , Introductory linguistics, New
     York: Chilton Books, 1964, p. 67.
161. Jesperson, 1921, pp. 241-242.
162. Sapir, 1929, p. 212.
163. See Ellis and Abarbanel for bibliography.
164. Samuel E. Martin, "Speech levels in Japan and Korea, "
     in Dell Hymes, pp. 407-415. See also Roy
     Andrew Miller, The Japanese language, Chicago:
     University of Chicago Press, 1967, pp. 277-286.
165. Shuy.
166. Roger D. Abrahams, Deep down in the jungle, Hatboro,
     Pa. : Folklore Associates, 1964, p. 36. Ulf
     Hannerz, Soulside, New York: Columbia Univer-
     sity Press, 1969, p. 95. Frank Riessman, "The
     culture of the underprivileged, " in Staten W.
     Webster, ed. , The disadvantaged learner, San
     Francisco: Chandler Pub. Co. , 1966, pp. 53-61.

Walter A. Wolfram, A sociolinguistic description
of Detroit Negro speech, Washington, D. C. :
Center for Applied Linguistics, 1969.

167. Gunnar Myrdal, An American dilemma, New York:
Harper and Row, [1944] 1962, pp. 1073-1078.
Helen Hacker also compares the "Castelike Sta-
tus of Women and Negroes" in a well-developed
chart, in "Women as a minority group, " Social
Forces, 30 (October 1951), pp. 60-69.

168. Webster's third international dictionary.

CHAPTER XI

169. The material in this chapter also occurs in my book
on nonverbal communication, Key, 1974, Chapter
VIII, "Dialects of nonverbal behavior and special
message systems. "

170. Weston LaBarre used the term "body language" in an
early article, "The cultural basis of emotions
and gestures, " Journal of Personality, 16:1
(September 1947), also in Bobbs-Merrill Reprint
Series S-157, also in D. G. Haring, ed. , Personal character and cultural milieu, Syracuse,
N. Y. : Syracuse University Press, 1956.

171. George L. Trager, "Paralanguage: a first approxima-
tion, " Studies in Linguistics, 13 (1958), pp. 1-
12. Reprinted in Hymes, 1964.

172. The term "kinesics" was introduced by Ray L. Birdwhistell in 1952. See Kinesics and context,
Philadelphia: University of Pennsylvania Press,
1970.

173. William Wells Newell; Games and songs of American
children [1883], reprinted by Dover Publications,
New York, 1963, pp. 5-6.

174. Los Angeles Times, April 25, 1966.

175. George M. Cowan, "Mazateco whistle speech, " Language
24 (1948), Reprinted in Hymes, 1964.

176. Alfred S. Hayes, "A tentative schematization for research in the teaching of cross-cultural communication, " International Journal of American Linguistics, 28:1 (Pt. II), (January 1962), pp. 155-
167.

177. Carroll L. Olsen, "Voice register and intonation levels
in two dialects of Spanish, " paper read at the
Modern Language Association, 1972.

178. Floyd M. Cammack and Hildebert Van Buren, "Paralan-

guage across cultures," The English Language
       Education Council, Bulletin, 22 (November 1967),
       p. 8.
179. Henry Balfour, "Ritual and secular uses of vibrating
       membranes as voice-disguisers," Journal of the
       Royal Anthropological Institute of Great Britain
       and Ireland, 78 (1948), pp. 45-69.
180. William J. Samarin, The Gbeya language, Berkeley:
       University of California Press, 1966, p. 39.
181. George Devereux, "Mohave voice and speech manner-
       isms," Word, 5:3 (1949), reprinted in Hymes,
       1964.
182. Adam Kendon and Andrew Ferber, "A description of
       some human greetings," in R. P. Michael and
       J. H. Crook, eds., Comparative ecology and
       behaviour of primates, London: Academic Press,
       1973.
183. Dick and Jane as victims, Women on Words and Images,
       Princeton, N.J., 1972, p. 40.
184. Argyle, et al.   ..
185. Werner Beinhauer, "Uber 'Piropos': eine Studie über
       spanische Liebessprache," Volkstum und Kultur
       der Romanen, 7 (1934), pp. 111-163.
186. Shulamith Firestone, The dialectic of sex. New York:
       William Morrow, 1970, pp. 101-102.
187. Jane van Lawick-Goodall, In the shadow of man, Boston:
       Houghton Mifflin, 1971, p. 81.
188. Ashley Montagu, Touching: the human significance of
       the skin, New York: Columbia University Press,
       1971, p. 208.
189. Richard Brilliant, Gesture and rank in Roman art, New
       Haven, Conn.: The Academy, 1963.
190. Peter F. Ostwald, "Human sounds," in Dominick A.
       Barbara, ed., Psychological and psychiatric
       aspects of speech and hearing, 1960, p. 126.
191. Ian Hindmarch, "Pupil size and non-verbal communi-
       cation," in NATO Symposium on nonverbal com-
       munication, eds. Michael Argyle and Ralph
       Exline, Wadham College, Oxford, 1969, p. 26.
192. Birdwhistell, p. 159.

                              CHAPTER XII

193. Ann Stanford, ed., The women poets in English: an
       anthology, New York: McGraw-Hill, 1972, p.
       xxxvii. Robert Hutchinson, ed., Poems of

Anne Bradstreet, New York: Dover Publications, 1969, p. 13.

194. Quoted in Ann Stanford, "Anne Bradstreet...," The New England Quarterly, 39:3 (September 1966), p. 375.

195. Hutchinson (see note 193), p. 9.

196. Woolf, p. 65. See also quotations in Adburgham.

197. Ann Stanford, ed., The Women Poets ... (see note 193), p. xxxvi.

198. Carol Ohmann, "Emily Brontë in the hands of male critics," College English, 32:8 (May 1971), pp. 906-913. Especially pp. 906 and 908.

199. Greene, especially p. 63.

200. Greene, pp. 66-67.

201. Woolf, p. 64.

202. Herbert Marder, Feminism and art: a study of Virginia Woolf, Chicago: University of Chicago Press, 1968, pp. 14-15.

203. Gilbert K. Chesterton, The Victorian age in literature, Oxford University Press, 1966, p. 48.

204. Noel Gilroy Annan, Leslie Stephen: his thought and character in relation to his time, Cambridge, Mass.: Harvard University Press, 1952, p. 226.

205. Woolf, p. 181.

206. W. G. Aston, A history of Japanese literature, London, 1907, 410 pp. Donald Keene, Japanese literature, New York: Grove Press, 1955, pp. 67-73. The Kokusai Bunka Shinkokai, ed., Introduction to Classic Japanese literature, Tokyo: Kokusai Bunka Shinkokai (Society for International Cultural Relations), 1948, p. 443. Roy Andrew Miller, The Japanese language, Chicago: University of Chicago Press, 1967, pp. 38-39.

207. Aston (see note 206), pp. 55-56.

208. Aston, p. 232.

209. Encyclopaedia Britannica, Vol. 5, "Chinese literature," 1965.

210. Woolf, p. 80.

211. C. R. MacKinnon of Dunakin, The Highlands in history, Glasgow: Collins, 1961, p. 82.

212. Samuel Butler, see Bibliography.

213. Woolf, pp. 51-52.

214. Los Angeles Times, November 7, 1972.

215. Florence Howe, "Identity and expression: a writing course for women" (mimeo.), p. 4.

216. Goldberg.

217.   Lawrence Kohlberg, "A cognitive-developmental analysis
          of children's sex-role concepts and attitudes,"
          in Eleanor Maccoby, ed., The development of
          sex differences, Palo Alto, Cal.: Stanford Uni-
          versity Press, 1966.
218.   Woolf, p. 91.
219.   Quoted from Mrs. Leslie Stephen, Notes from sick
          rooms, 1883, p. 5, in Noel Gilroy Annan, Les-
          lie Stephen: his thought and character in rela-
          tion to his time, Cambridge, Mass.: Harvard
          University Press, 1952, p. 100.
220.   Winifred Holtby, Virginia Woolf, London: Wishart and
          Co., 1932, pp. 12-14.
221.   George K. Anderson, Old and Middle English literature
          from the beginnings to 1485, New York: Collier
          Books, 1962, p. 18.
222.   Jack Hamilton, "A conversation with Jane Austen,"
          Intellectual Digest (May 1973), p. 17.
223.   Baecklund, p. 19.
224.   Bernice Sandler, et al., "Women in the curriculum,"
          Project on the Status and Education of Women,
          Association of American Colleges, 1818 R Street,
          N. W., Washington, D. C. 20009, November
          1972, p. 2.
225.   Woolf, pp. 45-46.
226.   D. H. Lawrence, Lady Chatterley's Lover, New York:
          Grove Press, 1962.
227.   The remarks following are taken from my article,
          "The role of male and female in children's
          books," Wilson Library Bulletin, 46:2 (October
          1971), pp. 174-175.
228.   Pearl S. Buck, East and West and the novel, Peking,
          1932, pp. 4-5, 24.
229.   Francis L. K. Hsu, Americans and Chinese: two ways
          of life, New York: Henry Schuman, 1953, pp.
          23-25.
230.   Caroline Bird, Born female: the high cost of keeping
          women down, New York: David McKay, 1968,
          p. 27.   See also Adburgham.

CHAPTER XIII

231.   Ajax, line 293.
232.   Key, 1974, Chapter V, "The function of silence in non-
          verbal communication."
233.   Sidney J. Baker, "Autonomic resistances in word asso-

ciation tests," Psychoanalytic Quarterly, 20 (1951), pp. 275-283.

234. Ralph G. Martin, Jennie: the life of Lady Randolph Churchill: the romantic years 1854-1895, Englewood Cliffs, N. J.: Prentice-Hall, 1969, p. 143.

235. The Oxford Dictionary of Quotations, New York: Oxford University Press, 1955, p. 280.

236. See Olsen, who discusses why writers don't write.

237. Sir James George Frazer, Folk-lore in the Old Testament: studies in comparative religion, legend and law, Vol. 3, London: Macmillan, 1919, pp. 71-81.

238. Sapir, 1915, p. 179.

239. Corinne Geeting, "The tyranny of women's liberation," ETC: A review of General Semantics, 28:3 (September 1971), pp. 358-359.

240. Zimmerman and West. The other study was a student paper by Kester.

241. Michael Argyle, Mansur Lalljee, and Mark Cook, "The effects of visibility on interaction in a dyad," Human Relations, 21:1 (February 1968), p. 15.

242. Gleason.

243. Barbara Bellow Watson, A Shavian guide to the intelligent woman, New York: W. W. Norton, 1964, p. 189.

244. "Shaw at Peak," Book Selection, Intellectual Digest (January 1973), p. 27.

CHAPTER XIV

245. Jespersen, 1921, p. 242.

246. Jespersen, 1921, p. 244. For sound change in the Spanish language see Gregorio Salvador, "Fonética masculina y fonética femenina en el habla de Vertientes y Tarifa (Granada), in Sever Pop., ed., Orbis, 1:1 (1952), pp. 19-24.

247. Harvey Wish, Society and thought in early America, New York: David McKay, 1950, p. 573.

248. Andre Martinet, A functional view of language, New York: Oxford University Press, 1962, pp. 15-19.

249. Rothstein.

250. Blood.

251. Henry M. Hoenigswald, "Are there universals of linguistic change?" in Joseph H. Greenberg, Universals of language, Chapter 2, Cambridge, Mass.

MIT Press, 1963, pp. 23-41.

252. Harry H. Johnston, A comparative study of the Bantu
      and Semi Bantu languages, London: Oxford Uni-
      versity Press, 1922, Vol. II, p. 89.

253. This information was given to me by Douglas Taylor
      in correspondence. Taylor has published ex-
      tensively on the linguistics of this area and has
      a book in progress on these aspects.

254. Joan Rubin, "Bilingualism in Paraguay," Anthropolo-
      gical Linguistics, 4:1 (1962), pp. 52-58.

255. William J. Samarin, Field linguistics, New York: Holt,
      Rinehart and Winston, 1967, p. 62.

                        CHAPTER XV

256. Spokeswoman, 1:4 (August 28, 1970), p. 5.

257. Scott, Foresman, 1972.

258. Anon., "Guidelines...," (see note 257), pp. 6-7.

259. Gardner, Bosmajian, and Sutton.

260. Uriel Weinreich, William Labov, and Marvin I. Herzog,
      "Empirical foundations for a theory of language
      change," in W. P. Lehmann and Yakov Malkiel,
      eds., Directions for Historical Linguistics, Aus-
      tin: University of Texas Press, 1968, pp. 183-
      187.

261. U. R. Ehrenfels, "The common elements in the phi-
      losophy of matrilinear societies in India," in
      F. S. C. Northrop and Helen H. Livingston, eds.,
      Cross-cultural understanding: epistemology in
      anthropology, New York: Harper and Row, 1964,
      pp. 105-124.

262. Clare Boothe Luce, "Woman: A technological castaway,"
      Britannica Book of the Year 1973, p. 29.

263. Lady Chatterley's Lover, Introduction by Mark Schorer,
      New York: Grove Press, 1957, p. 13.

264. Robert Graves, 1965, p. 101.

265. Heilbrun, p. 100.

266. Dallas Kenmare, The nature of genius, London: P.
      Owen, 1960, p. 94; who paraphrased John Mac-
      murray, reason and emotion, London: Faber
      and Faber, 1935.

267. Specimens of the table talk of the late Samuel Taylor
      Coleridge, Vol II, London, 1835, p. 96.

268. Woolf, pp. 102-103. For more historical information
      on the androgynous concept see Ruth Gruber,

Virginia Woolf: a study, Leipzig: Bernhard Tauchnitz, 1935, pp. 86-87.

269. Carol Ohmann, "Emily Brontë in the hands of male critics," College English, 32:8 (May 1971), p. 907.

270. Quoted in Barbara Bellow Watson, A Shavian guide to the intelligent woman, New York: W. W. Norton, 1964, p. 21.

271. George Bernard Shaw, "The problem play--a symposium," in James B. Hall and Barry Ulanov, eds., Modern culture and the arts, New York: McGraw-Hill, 1967, pp. 346.

272. Quoted in Watson (see note 270), p. 23.

BIBLIOGRAPHY

This bibliography on the linguistic behavior of male and female is as complete as possible. It includes items of nonverbal and sociolinguistic interest when they have communicative focus. Most of the items are language oriented but I have included a few more general references which have deeply influenced this book, such as de Beauvoir, Graves, Mead, Whorf, and Woolf. Also I have included a few marginal references from literature when they dealt with the use of language as I have treated it in this book. The matter of gender is only touched upon; another bibliography could be constructed on just that aspect of language.

Ackerman, Louise M.
    1962   " 'Lady' as a synonym for 'woman', " American
            Speech 37:3, 284-85.

Adam, Lucien
    1879   "Du parler des hommes et du parler des fem-
            mes dans la langue Caraïbe, " Memoires 1878,
            Academie de Stanislaus, Paris, 145-176.

Adam, Lucien, and V. Henry
    1880   Arte y vocabulario de la lengua chiquita,
            Paris, vi-vii, 4-8.

Adburgham, Alison
    1972   Women in print: writing women and women's
            magazines from the restoration to the acces-
            sion of Victoria, London: George Allen and
            Unwin.

Altshuler, Nathan
    1956   "Linguistic forms as symbols of people, "
            International Journal of American Linguistics
            22:2, 106-112. (See comments in H. A. Glea-
            son, Jr. , "Comparison of linguistic systems, "
            International Journal of American Linguistics,
            22:4 (October 1956), pp. 273-275; William J.
            Samarin, Field Linguistics, New York: Holt,
            Rinehart and Winston, 1967, p. 109.)

Altus, William D.

1959   "Sexual role, the short story, and the writer,"
          Journal of Psychology 47, 37-40.
Argyle, Michael, Mansur Lalljee, and Mark Cook
1968   "The effects of visibility on interaction in a
          dyad," Human Relations 21:1 (February), p.
          15.
Atwood, E. Bagby
1950   "The pronunciation of 'Mrs. ', " American
          Speech 25, 10-18.
Austin, William M.
1965   "Some social aspects of paralanguage," Cana-
          dian Journal of Linguistics 11:1, 31-39.
Baecklund, Astrid
1956   "The names of women in medieval Novgorod",
          For Roman Jakobson, The Hague: Mouton,
          19-24.
Baron, Naomi
1971   "A reanalysis of English grammatical gender",
          Lingua 27 (August), 113-140.
Barron, Nancy
1970   "Grammatical case and sex role: language
          differences in interaction", Diss. University
          of Missouri.
1971   "Sex-typed language: the production of gram-
          matical cases," Acta Sociologica 14:2, 24-42.
Bayer, Ann
1970   "A women's lib exposé of male villainy, "
          Life, August 7, 62A-64.
Beauvoir, Simone de
1953   The second sex, New York: Knopf, 1953; Ban-
          tam, 1965.
Bernard, Jessie
1968   "Talk, conversation, listening, silence," The
          Sex Game, Englewood Cliffs, N. J.: Prentice-
          Hall, 135-164.
Birdwhistell, Ray L.
1970   "Masculinity and femininity as display," in
          Kinesics and context: essays on body motion
          communication, Philadelphia: University of
          Pennsylvania Press, 39-46.
Blanchard, Irene
1970   "Genetic development of consonant sounds in
          children's speech," Actes du Xe Congres In-
          ternational des Linguistes, 1967, Vol. III,
          Bucharest, 145-49.
Blood, Doris
1962   "Women's speech characteristics in Cham, "

    Asian Culture 3:3-4, 139-143.
Boas, Franz, ed.
    Handbook of American Indian languages, Vol.
    1, 1911; Vol 2, 1922; Vol. 3, 1934, Bureau
    of American Ethnology, Bulletin 40.
Bodine, Ann [Rutgers University]
    1973   "Sex differentiation in language, " paper read
            at the Symposium on Women and Language,
            Rutgers University.
Bogoras, Waldemar
    1922   "Chukchee" in Boas, q. v.
Bosmajian, Haig A.
    1972   "The language of sexism, " ETC 29:3 (Septem-
            ber), 305-313. Reprinted in Reflections.
Bostrom, Robert N. , and Alan P. Kemp
    1969   "Type of speech, sex of speaker, and sex of
            subject as factors influencing persuasion, "
            Central States Speech Journal, (Winter) 245-
            251.
Bratkowsky, Joan [Univ. of Indiana]
    n. d.   "A cross-linguistic comparison of designations
            for female human beings, " 27 pages.
    1973   "A cross-linguistic study of sex-marked gen-
            ders, " 46 pages.
Brend, Ruth M.
    1971   "Male-female differences in American English
            intonation, " 7th International Congress of Pho-
            netic Sciences, Canada, 1971.
Brêton, Raymond
    1665   Dictionaire Caraibe-Francois, Auxerre, re-
            printed by Jules Platzmann, 1892.
    1666   Dictionaire Francois-Caraibe, Auxerre, re-
            printed by Jules Platzmann, Leipzig, 1900.
Brooks, Maria Z. , and Kenneth L. Nalibow
    1970   "The gender of referentials in Polish, " Inter-
            national Journal of Slavic Linguistics and Po-
            etics 13, 136-142.
Bugental, Daphne E. , Leonore R. Love, and Robert M.
    Gianetto
    1971   "Perfidious feminine faces, " Journal of Per-
            sonality and Social Psychology 17:3, 314-318.
Burr, Elizabeth, Susan Dunn, and Norma Farquhar
    1972   "Women and the language of inequality, " So-
            cial education 36:8, (December) 841-845.
    1973   "Guidelines for equal treatment of the sexes
            in social studies textbooks, " Westside Women's
            Committee, P. O. Box 24 D 20, Los Angeles,

California 90024.

Butler, Samuel
1897   The authoress of the Odyssey: where and when
          she wrote, who she was, the use she made of
          the Iliad, and how the poem grew under her
          hands, with a new introduction by David Grene,
          Chicago: University of Chicago Press, 1967.

Callery, R. E. [Northern Illinois Univ.]
1973   "Dialectal variation in terms for men and
          women," paper read at the Midwest Regional
          American Dialect Society, Chicago.
Chamberlain, Alexander F.
1912   "Women's languages," American Anthropologist
          14, 579-581.
Cherry, Louise [Harvard Univ.]
          "Sex differences in verbal interaction of pre-
          school teachers and children," dissertation in
          progress.

Cleve
1904   "Uber die Frauensprache" [part of a larger
          article], Zeitschrift für Ethnologie 36, 460-
          463.

Cohen, Marcel
1956   "L'entrée dans le groupe et le langage"
          [from Part II], Chapter I in Pour une socio-
          logie du langage, Paris: Paris Editions,
          Albin Michel, 112-121.
Conklin, Nancy Faires [Univ. of Michigan]
1973   "Perspectives on the dialects of women,"
          paper read at the Midwest Regional American
          Dialect Society, Michigan.
1974   "Toward a feminist analysis of linguistic be-
          havior," University of Michigan papers in
          women's studies 1:1, February (Ann Arbor),
          pp. 51-73.

Connors, Kathleen
1971   "Studies in feminine agentives in selected
          European languages," Romance philology 24:
          4, May, 573-598.
Converse, Charles Crozat
1884   "A new pronoun," The critic and good litera-
          ture 4 (August 2), p. 55; [letters to the edi-
          tor] The Critic 5 (August 16), pp. 79-80.
1889   "That desired impersonal pronoun," The
          Writer 3, 247-248.

Coser, Rose Laub
    1960   "Laughter among colleagues, " Psychiatry 23
                (February), pp. 81-95.

Cosper, Wilma Baker
    1971   "An analysis of sex differences in teacher-
                student interaction as manifest in verbal and
                nonverbal behavior cues, " Dissertation Ab-
                stracts 32. 1-A 302 (July) University of Ten-
                nessee.

Densmore, Dana
                "Speech is the form of thought, " 10 pages.
                KNOW, Inc. P. O. Box 10197, Pittsburgh,
                Pa. 15232.
"Down with Manglish?" 1972 Junior Scholastic (January 17),
                p. 3.

Eble, Connie C. [Univ. of North Carolina]
    1972   "How the speech of some is more equal than
                others, " paper read at the Southeastern Con-
                ference on Linguistics (SECOL), SECOL VIII,
                1972 (Chapel Hill: University of North Caro-
                lina).
    1972   "If ladies weren't present, I'd tell you what
                I really think, " paper read at the South Atlan-
                tic Regional American Dialect Society.

Ehrenreich, Paul
    1894   "Materialien zur Sprachenkunde Brasiliens: I,
                Die Sprache der Caraya (Goyaz), " Zeitschrift
                für Ethnologie 26, 20-37; 49-60.

Ekka, Francis
    1972   "Men's and women's speech in Kūṟux, " Lin-
                guistics 81, 25-31.

Ell, Marilou [Michigan State University]
    1972   "The voice of authority: women's intonation
                patterns. "

Ellis, Albert, and Albert Abarbanel, eds.
    1961   "Language and Sex, " The encyclopedia of sex-
                ual behavior, Vol. II, 585-598.

Erades, P. A.
    1956   "Contributions to Modern English syntax: V.
                A note on gender, " Moderna Språk 50, 2-11.

Ervin, Susan M.
    1962   "The connotations of gender, " Word 18, 249-
                261.

Farquhar, Norma, Susan Dunn, and Elizabeth Burr
    1972   "Sex stereotypes in elementary and secondary
            education, " Westside Women's Committee, P.
            O. Box 24D 20, Los Angeles, Ca. 90024.
Farwell, Marilyn
    19??   "Women and language, " in Jean Ramage Lep-
            paluoto, et al., eds., Women on the move: a
            feminist perspective (KNOW, Inc., P. O. Box
            10197, Pittsburgh, Pa. 15232).
Faust, Jean
    1970   "Words that oppress, " Women Speaking, re-
            print available from KNOW, Inc., P. O. Box
            10197, Pittsburgh, Pa. 15232.
Faust, Norma
    1963   "El lenguaje de los hombres y mujeres en
            Cocama, " Peru Indigena 10, 115-17.
Feminist Writers Workshop
    1973   An intelligent woman's guide to dirty words:
            English words and phrases reflecting sexist
            attitudes toward women in patriarchal society,
            comp. by the Feminist Writers Workshop,
            commentaries by Ruth Todasco, Jessie Sher-
            idan, Ellen Morgan, Kathryn Starr, Chicago:
            Young Women's Christian Association, Loop
            Center.
Fessler, Robert W. [University of Maryland]
    1972   "Men and women: who talks most?", 16 pages.
Fischer, John L.
    1958   "Social influences on the choice of a linguistic
            variant, " Word 14, pp. 45-56, reprinted in
            Hymes, q. v., 483-88
Flannery, Regina
    1946   "Men's and women's speech in Gros Ventre, "
            International Journal of American Linguistics
            12:3, 133-35.
Fodor, István
    1959   "The origin of grammatical gender, " Lingua
            8, 1-41, 186-214.
Frazer, Sir James George
    1900   "A suggestion as to the origin of gender in
            language, " Fortnightly (Review) 73 (January),
            79-90.
Freeman, Jo
    n. d.   "The building of the gilded cage, " reprint a-
            vailable from KNOW, Inc., P. O. Box 10197,
            Pittsburgh, Pa. 15232.

Funk, Wilfred
    1950   "Romantic stories of words about women, "
            Chapter 15 in Word origins and their romantic
            stories, New York: Grosset and Dunlap, 247-
            253.
Furfey, Paul Hanly
    1944   "Men's and Women's language, " The American
            Catholic Sociological Review 5, 218-223.
    1944   "The semantic and grammatical principles in
            linguistic analysis, " Studies in Linguistics 2:
            3, 56-66.

Gardner, Gerald H. F.
    1970   "The changing role of men in the changing
            world of women, " paper read at the American
            Psychological Association, Miami.   Reprint
            available from KNOW, Inc., P. O. Box 10197,
            Pittsburgh, Pa. 15232.
Gary, Sandra
    1972   "What are we talking about?" Ms. Magazine
            (December), 72-73, 99.
George, Mary Lee
    1972   "What's in a word?" and "Alternatives to sex-
            ist language, " in Sexism in education, Emma
            Willard Task Force on Education, University
            Station Box No. 14229, Minneapolis, Minn.
            55414.
Gilley, Hoyt Melvyn, and Collier Stephen Summers
    1970   "Sex differences in the use of hostile verbs, "
            Journal of Psychology 76, 33-37.
Gleason, Jean Berko [Boston Univ., Psych.]
    n. d.   "Code-switching in children's language, " W.
            Wolck, ed., New York: Academic Press.
    1974   "Father's language" [lecture at Stanford in the
            Child Language Lunches]
Goldberg, Philip
    1968   "Are women prejudiced against women?"
            Trans-action 5:5 (April), 28-30. Reprinted in
            Constantina Safilios-Rothschild, ed., Toward
            a sociology of women, Lexington, Mass.:
            Xerox College Publishing, 1972, pp. 10-13.
Graham, Alma
    1973   "The making of a nonsexist dictionary, " Ms.
            Magazine (December), pp. 12-14, 16 [on the
            making of the children's wordbook by American
            Heritage Publishing Co.; see also Trombley].

Grahame, Kenneth
    1899   "What they talked about" The Golden Age,
            New York: John Lane, pp. 133-139.
Grasserie, Raoul de la
    1909   "De la gynoglose (langage de sexe à sexe), "
            Des parler des differentes classes sociales,
            Paris, 330-34.
Graves, Robert
    1965   Mammon and the black goddess, New York:
            Doubleday.
Greene, Elsa
    1972   "Emily Dickinson was a poetess, " College
            English 34:1, 63-70.
Greer, Germaine
    1971   "Abuse, " The female eunuch, New York: Mc-
            Graw-Hill, 259-269.
Gunderson, Doris V.
    1972   "Sex roles in reading, " ERIC ED 064 671
            EDRS.

Haas, Mary R.
    1944   "Men's and women's speech in Koasati, " Lan-
            guage 20:3, 142-49. Reprinted in Hymes, q. v.,
            228-233.
Hage, Dorothy
    1972   "There's glory for you, " Aphra 3:3 (Summer),
            2-14.
Hall, Robert A. , Jr.
    1951   "Sex reference and grammatical gender in
            English, " American Speech 26:3 (October),
            170-72.
Hancock, Cecily Raysor
    1963   " 'Lady' and 'Woman', " American Speech 38
            (October), 234-35.
Harrington, John P.
    1944   "Ten ways in which the study of South Ameri-
            can languages illuminates linguistic knowledge, "
            Acta Americana 2, 104-108.
Heilbrun, Carolyn G.
    1964   Toward a recognition of androgyny, New York:
            Knopf, [1973].
Henley, Nancy
    1972   "The politics of touch, " Women: A Journal of
            Liberation 3:1, 7-8.
    1973   "Power, sex, and nonverbal communication, "
            Berkeley Journal of Sociology 18, pp. 1-26.

1973   "Status and sex: some touching observations, " Bulletin of the Psychonomic Society 2:2 (August), 91-93.

Henry, V.
1879   "Sur le parler des hommes et le parler des femmes dans la langue chiquita, " Revue de Linguistique et de Philologie Comparée 12, 305-313.

Hernando Balmori, Clemente
1967   Estudios de área lingüística indígena, Centro de Estudios Lingüísticos, Vol. 3, Universidad de Buenos Aires.

Hirschman, Lynette
1973   "Female-male differences in conversational interaction, " paper read at the Linguistic Society of America, San Diego.

Hoffman, Nicholas von
n. d.   "Misogyny in everyday life, " reprint available from KNOW, Inc., P. O. Box 10197, Pittsburgh, Pa. 15232.

Hogan, Helen
1971   "The ethnography of speaking among the Ashanti, " Texas working papers in sociolinguistics 1.

Hole, Judith, and Ellen Levine
1971   "The politics of language, " in Rebirth of feminism (New York: Quadrangle Books), pp. 222-225.

Howard, Pamela
1972   "Watch your language, men, " More: A Journalism Review 2:2 (February), pp. 3-4.

Hymes, Dell
1964   Language in culture and society: a reader in linguistics and anthropology, New York: Harper and Row.

Jakobson, Roman
1960   "The gender pattern of Russian, " Studii si Cercetări Lingvistice 11:3, 541-43.

James, Henry
1907   "The Speech of American women, " Harper's Bazaar 41, 113-17.

Jespersen, Otto
1921   "The Woman, " Chapter 13 in Language: its nature, development and origin, New York: W. W. Norton, 237-254.

1924   "Sex and gender, " Chapter 17 in The philosophy of grammar, New York: W. W. Norton,
226-243.

1933   "Gender, " Chapter 19 in Essentials of English
grammar, University, University of Alabama
Press [1964], 188-196.

Jones, Charles
1967   "The grammatical category of gender in Early
Middle English, " English Studies 48, 289-305.

Kagan, Jerome
1964   "Acquisition and significance of sex typing and
sex role identity, " in Martin L. Hoffman and
Lois Wladis Hoffman, eds. , Review of child
development research, Vol. I, Russell Sage
Foundation, 137-167.

Keenan, Elinor
in pr.   "Norm-makers, norm-breakers: uses of speech
by men and women in a Malagasy community, "
in R. Baumann and J. F. Sherzer, eds. , Ex-
plorations in the ethnography of speaking (Cambridge, Eng. : Cambridge University Press).

Kelly, Edward Hanford
1969   "A 'bitch' by any other name is less poetic, "
Word Study 45:1 (October), 1-4.

Kester, Judy [California State Univ. , San Jose]
n. d.   "Why women talk that way: cultural influences
on male-female verbal behavior, " 25 pages.

Key, Mary Ritchie
1970   "Linguistic behavior of male and female"
[course outline and bibliography] in Florence
Howe, ed. , Female studies: No. 2, Commission on the Status of Women, Modern Language Association, distributed by KNOW, Inc. ,
P. O. Box 10197, Pittsburgh, Pa. 15232.

1971   "The role of male and female in children's
books, " Wilson Library Bulletin 46:2 (October),
167-176.

1972   "Linguistic behavior of male and female, "
Linguistics 88 (August), 15-31.

1975   "Dialects of nonverbal behavior: special message systems, " Chapter VIII in Paralanguage
and kinesics, Metuchen, N. J. : Scarecrow
Press.

Koppelman Cornillon, J.
1973   "Teaching about sexist language in a first year

college composition course, " paper read at
the Midwest Modern Language Association.
Kramer, Cheris [Univ. of Illinois at Urbana, Speech]
    1973   "Women's rhetoric in New Yorker cartoons:
patterns for a Mildred Milquetoast, " paper
read at the Speech Communication Association
Convention, November, 1973.
    1974   "Women's speech: separate but unequal?"
Quarterly Journal of Speech 60:1, February,
14-24.
Kraus, Flora
    1924   "Die Frauensprache bei den primitiven Völ-
kern, " Imago 10:215, 296-313.
Krause, Fritz
    1911   In den Wildnissen Brasiliens: Bericht und
Ergebnisse der Leipziger Araguaya-Expedi-
tion 1908, Leipzig, 60-61, 342-344, 416-457.
Kröll, Heinz
    1953   "Termes désignant les seins de la femme en
portugais, " Orbis 2, 19-32.

Lakoff, Robin
    1973   "Language and woman's place, " Language in
Society 2:1 (April), 45-80.
Landis, M. H., and H. E. Burtt
    1924   "A study of conversations, " Journal of Com-
parative Psychology 4, 81-89.
Langenfelt, Gösta
    1951   "She and her instead of it and its, " Anglia
70:1, 90-101.
Lasch, Richard
    1907   "Uber Sondersprachen und ihre Entstehung:
I. Frauensprachen, " Anthropologische Gesell-
schaft in Vienna. Mitteil. 37, 89-101.
Lennert, Midge, and Norma Willson
    1973   A woman's new world dictionary (51% Publi-
cations, Box 371, Lomita, Cal. 90717).
Lévy, Ernest-Henri
    1924   "Langue des homme et langue des femmes en
Judéo-Allemand, " Melanges: offerts à M.
Charles Andler par ses amis et ses eleves,
University of Strasbourg, Publications de la
Faculté des lettres de l'université de Stras-
bourg, Fasc. 21, 197-215.
Lewis, Michael
    1972   "Culture and gender roles: there's no unisex

in the nursery," Psychology Today, May, 54-
57.

McKissick, Dorothy [University of California at Los Angeles--
    Sociology]
    1973   "Language, sex roles and women's self con-
             cept. "
Malone, Sister Helen Daniel
    1954   "An analysis and evaluation of phonemic differ-
             ences in the speech of boys and girls at the
             kindergarten, first, second, and third grade
             levels," dissertation, University of Michigan.
Markel, Norman N., Layne D. Prebor, and John F. Brandt
    1972   "Bio-social factors in dyadic communication:
             sex and speaking intensity," Journal of Per-
             sonality and Social Psychology 23, 11-13.
Martinet, André
    1962   A functional view of language, New York: Ox-
             ford University Press, 15-19.
    1971   "Feminine gender," lecture at University of
             California at Berkeley.
Mass Media Associates
    n. d.   "Included Out" [a short film cartoon on sexist
             language in religion, generic terms]. The
             Associates, 1720 Chouteau Ave., St. Louis,
             Mo. 63103
Mattingly, Ignatius G.
    1966   "Speaker variation and vocal-tract size," Jour-
             nal of the Acoustical Society of America 39:6
             (June), 1219.
Mauss, Marcel
    1923   "On language and primitive forms of classifi-
             cation" [translation], Journal de Psychologie:
             Normale et Pathologique 20, 944-947. Re-
             printed in A. Meillet, Linguistique historique
             et linguistique generale, Paris, 1938-1948,
             and Hymes, q. v., pp. 125-127.
Mead, Margaret
    1935   Sex and temperament in three primitive socie-
             ties, New York: Dell Pub. Co. [1968].
    1949   Male and female: a study of the sexes in a
             changing world, New York: William Morrow
             [1967].
Meillet, A.
    1923   "The feminine gender in the Indo-European lan-
             guages" ("Le genre feminin dans les langues

Indo-Européennes"), Journal de Psychologie:
Normale et Pathologique 20, 943-44, reprinted
in Hymes, q. v., 124; also in Meillet, A.,
Linguistique historique et linguistique generale,
Paris, 1926-1936, Vol. II, 24-28.

Meredith, Mamie
    1930   " 'Doctresses', 'Authoresses', and others, "
            American Speech 5:6 (August), 476-481.
    1951   "The language of feminine fashions, " American
            Speech 26:3 (October), 231-32.

Michalsen, Tonje, and Svatopluk Štech, Jr.
    1962   "A few remarks on the so-called emotive femi-
            nine in Czech, " Scando-Slavica 8, 182-190.

Miller, Casey, and Kate Swift [sic]
    1972   "One small step for genkind, " The New York
            Times Magazine, April 16, 1972, 36, 99-101,
            106, reprinted as "Is language sexist?" in
            Cosmopolitan (September), 89-92, 96.

Miller, Kate, and Casey Swift [sic]
    1972   "De-sexing the English language, " Ms: The
            New Magazine for Women, preview issue
            (Spring), 7.

"Miscellany: II. Mk., " 1941 American Speech 16, 229-230.

Moe, Albert F.
    1963   "'Lady' and 'Woman': the terms' use in the
            1880's, " American Speech 38:4 (December),
            295.

Moore, Samuel
    1921   "Grammatical and natural gender in Middle
            English, " Publications of the Modern Language
            Association 36, 79-103.

Murray, Jessica
    1972   "Male perspective in language, " Women: A
            Journal of Liberation 3:1, 46-50.

Musacchio, George L.
    1968   "Milton's feminine pronouns with neuter ante-
            cedents, " Journal of English Linguistics 2
            (March), 23-28.

Nichols, Patricia C. [California State Univ., San Jose]
    1972   "Gender in English: syntactic and semantic
            functions, " 12 pages.

Nicholson, Margaret
    1957   A dictionary of American-English usage: based
            on Fowler's Modern English usage, New York:

Oxford University Press.
Nilsen, Alleen Pace
   n. d.   "Sexism and language, " 5 pages.
   1972   "A semantic analysis of words in modern
           American English which display transparent
           incorporation of the features +masculine and
           +feminine. "
   1972   "Sexism in English: a feminist view, " Female
           studies VI, 102-109 (Old Westbury, N. Y. : The
           Feminist Press).
   1973   "The correlation between gender and other
           semantic features in American English, " paper
           read at the Linguistic Society of America,
           San Diego.
   1973   "Grammatical gender and its relationship to
           the equal treatment of males and females in
           children's books, " dissertation, University of
           Iowa.
Nilsen, Don and Alleen Nilsen [Arizona State University]
   n. d.   "Topless topography, " 4 pages.

O'Donnell, Holly Smith
   1973   "Sexism in language, " Elementary English
           50. 7, (October), 1067-1072.
Ohnuki-Tierney, Emiko
   1971   "The status of women and speech variation
           in Japan--a problem and method in sociolin-
           guistics, " paper read at the American Anthro-
           pologist Association, New York.
Olsen, Tillie
   1970   "Silences: when writers don't write, " Women:
           A Journal of Liberation 2:1 (Fall), 43-44.

Peisach, Estelle Cherry
   1965   "Children's comprehension of teacher and
           peer speech, " Child Development 36, 467-480.
Pop, Sever, ed.
   1952   "Le langage des femmes: enquête linguistique
           a l'échelle mondiale, " Orbis 1:1, 10-86; [2nd
           part] Orbis 2, 1953, 7-34.
Pottier, Bernard
   1972   "Langage des hommes et langage des femmes
           en cocama (tupi), " in Jacqueline M. C. Thomas
           and Lucien Bernot, eds. , Langues et tech-
           niques, nature et société, Paris, Klincksieck.

Récatas, Basile
    1934   "La femme et le bilinguisme, " Chapter III in
            L'état actuel du bilinguisme chez les Macédo-
            Roumains du Pinde et le rôle de la femme
            dans le langage, Paris: Librairie E. Droz
            18-28.

Reik, Theodor
    1954   "Men and women speak different languages, "
            Psychoanalysis Vol. 1-2, 3-15.

Rhome, Frances Dodson [Purdue University]
    1972   "Manglish: what's it all about?" paper read
            at the Midwest Modern Language Association,
            St. Louis.

Rosenfeld, Howard M.
    1966   "Approval-seeking and approval-inducing func-
            tions of verbal and nonverbal responses in the
            dyad, " Journal of Personality and Social Psy-
            chology 4:6, 597-605.

Ross, Alan S. C.
    1936   "Sex and gender in the Lindisfarne gospels, "
            Journal of English and Germanic Philology 35,
            321-330.

Rothstein, Robert A.
    1973   "Sex, gender and the October revolution, " in
            Stephen Anderson and Paul Kiparsky, eds. ,
            A festschrift for Morris Halle, New York:
            Holt, Rinehart and Winston.

Royen, Gerlach
    1929   Die nominalen Klassifikations-systeme in den
            Sprachen der Erde: Historisch-Kritische Stu-
            die, mit besonderer berücksichtigung des
            Indogermanischen, Anthropos-Bibliothek, Lin-
            guistische Band IV, Vienna, 1030 pages [re-
            view by Uhlenbeck, q. v.].

Rūke-Dravina, Velta
    1951   "Kā latvietēm rakstīt uzvārdus?" [Family
            name-forms for females] Latvju Zinas 491,
            3, 5.

Saada, Lucienne
    1970   "Le langage de femmes tunisiennes, " in David
            Cohen, ed. , Mélanges Marcel Cohen: etudes
            de linguistique, ethnographie et sciences con-
            nexes offertes par ses amis et ses élèves a
            l'occasion de son 80ème anniversaire, The
            Hague: Mouton, 320-325.

Sachs, Jacqueline, Philip Lieberman, and Donna Erickson
    1973   "Anatomical and cultural determinants of male
            and female speech, " in Roger W. Shuy and
            Ralph W. Fasold, eds., Language attitudes:
            current trends and prospects, Washington, D. C. :
            Georgetown University Press.
Saint-Jacques, Bernard
    1973   "Sex, dependency and language, " La linguist-
            ique 9. 1, 1973, 89-96.
Sanches, M. [University of Texas]
            "The acquisition of sex-role marking in the
            speech of Japanese children. "
Sapir, Edward
    1915   "Abnormal types of speech in Nootka, " re-
            printed in David G. Mandelbaum, ed. , Selected
            writings of Edward Sapir in language, culture
            and personality, Berkeley: University of Cal-
            ifornia Press, 1968, 179-196.
    1929   "Male and female forms of speech in Yana, "
            in St. W. J. Teeuwen, ed. , Donum natalicium
            schrijnen, Nijmegan-Utrecht: Dekker and Van
            de Vegt, 79-85, reprinted in Selected writings
            of Edward Sapir (see above), 206-212.
Sapper, Carl
    1897   "Mittelamericanische Caraiben, " International
            Archiv für Ethnographie 10, 53-60.
Scheflen, Albert E.
    1965   "Quasi-courtship behavior in psychotherapy, "
            Psychiatry 28, 245-257.
Schlauch, Margaret
    1936   "Recent Soviet studies in linguistics, " Science
            and Society: A Marxian Quarterly 1, 152-167.
            [Discusses Snegirev, q. v. , and feminine gen-
            der in the Zulu and Xosa languages.]

Schneider, Joseph W. , and Sally L. Hacker
    1973   "Sex role imagery and use of the generic 'man'
            in introductory texts: a case in the sociology
            of sociology, " The American Sociologist 8
            (February), 12-18.
Scholz, F.
    1965   "Genre, Genus und Person im Russischen, "
            Die Welt der Slaven 10, 281-304.
Schuell, Hildred
    1946   "Sex differences in relation to stuttering: part
            1, " Journal of Speech Disorders 11:4 (Decem-
            ber), 277-298.

Schulz, Muriel R. [California State Univ., Fullerton]
    1974   "The semantic derogation of woman," MS, 28 pages.
    1974   "Woman as 'Other' in language," MS, 17 pages.
Schwartz, Martin F.
    1968   "Identification of speaker sex from isolated, voiceless fricatives," Journal of the Acoustical Society of America 43:5, (May), 1178-79.
Schwartz, Martin F., and Helen E. Rine
    1968   "Identification of speaker sex from isolated whispered vowels," Journal of the Acoustical Society of America 44:6, 1736-37.
Scott, Foresman and Co.
    1972   "Guidelines for improving the image of women in textbooks," 9 pages.
Shenker, Israel
    1971   "Is it possible for a woman to manhandle the King's English?" New York Times, August 29, p. 58.
Sherzer, Joel
    1972   "Araucanian, South America," Texas working papers in sociolinguistics, Special number, Prolegomena to typologies of speech use, ed. by Regna Darnell, 43-46.
Shuster, Janet
    1973   "Grammatical forms marked for male and female in English," 5403 South Harper Avenue, Chicago.
    1974   "Verb forms of 'power and solidarity': sex as the basis of power."
Shuy, Roger W.
    1969   "Sex as a factor in sociolinguistic research" (mimeo., 15 pages), Center for Applied Linguistics, 1611 North Kent Street, Arlington, Va. 22209.
Silva Correia, João da
    1927   A linguagem da mulher, Academia das Ciencias de Lisboa, Biblioteca de Altos Estudios, Lisbon, 1935, 149 pages.
Silveira, Jeanette
    1972   "Thoughts on the politics of touch," Women's Press (Eugene, Ore.) 1:13 (February), 13.
Snegirev, I. L.
    1935   "Ob odnom vyraženii 'Ženskogo roda' v jazykay Zulu i Kosa" [On a certain expression for feminine gender in the Zulu and Xosa lan-

guages], Iazyk i Myshlenie 3-4, 281-284. [See
Schlauch].
Soskin, William F., and Vera P. John
     1963   "The study of spontaneous talk," in Roger G.
                  Barker, ed., The stream of behavior, New
                  York: Appleton-Century-Crofts, 228-281.
Spitzer, Leo
     1927   "Puxi, eine kleine Studie zur Sprache einer
                  Mutter: I," Jahrbuch für Philologie (Munich)
                  3, 35-54; II, 101-115, III, 170-183.
Stanchfield, Jo M. [Occidental College]
     n. d.   "The sexual factor in language development
                  and reading."
     1973   Sex differences in learning to read, Blooming-
                  ton, Ind. 47401: Phi Delta Kappa Educational
                  Foundation, 34 pages.
Stanley, Julia P. [Univ. of Georgia]
     1972   "The semantic features of the Machismo ethic
                  in English," paper read at the American Dia-
                  lect Society, New York.
Steadman, J. M., Jr.
     1938   "Affected and effeminate words," American
                  Speech 13:1 (February), 13-18.
Stene, Aasta
                  "The animate gender in modern colloquial
                  English," Norsk tidskrift for sprogvidenskap
                  7, 350-355.
Strainchamps, Ethel
     1971   "Our sexist language," Chapter 16 in Vivian
                  Gornick and Barbara K. Moran, eds., Woman
                  in sexist society: studies in power and power-
                  lessness, New York: Basic Books, 240-250.
Suardiaz, Delia E.
     1973   Sexism in the Spanish language, University of
                  Washington: Studies in Linguistics and Language
                  Learning, Vol. XI, 98 pages.
Sušnik, B. J. ed.
     19??   "Vocabularios inéditos de los idiomas Emok-
                  Toba y Choroti, recogidos por el Dr. Max
                  Schmidt," Boletín de la Sociedad Científica
                  del Paraguay y del Museo Etnográfico 6,
                  Asunción, pp. 1-32.
Sutton, William A. [Ball State Univ.]
     n. d.   "Guidelines relating to sexual fairness in lan-
                  guage."
     1973   "Sexual fairness in language," Muncie, Ind.
                  Ball State University, 12 pages.

Svartengren, T. Hilding
   1927   "The feminine gender for inanimate things in
            Anglo-American," American Speech 3:2 (De-
            cember), 83-113.
   1928-   "The use of the personal gender for inanimate
   1939   things," Dialect Notes, Vol. 6, 7-56.
   1954   "The use of feminine gender for inanimate
            things in American colloquial speech," Mod-
            erna Språk 48, 261-292.
Swacker, Marjorie
   1973   "Speaker-sex: a sociolinguistic variable,"
            paper read at the Linguistic Society of Ameri-
            ca, San Diego, California.

Tagliavini, Carlo
   1938   "Modificazioni del linguaggio nella parlata delle
            donne," Scritti in onore di Alfredo Trombetti,
            Milan: Ulrico Hoepli Editore, 87-142.
Taylor, Douglas
   1951   "Sex gender in Central American Carib," In-
            ternational Journal of American Linguistics
            17:2, 102-04.
   1970   [personal correspondence].
Templin, Mildred C.
   1966   "The study of articulation and language devel-
            opment during the early school years" in
            Frank Smith and George A. Miller, eds., The
            genesis of language: a psycholinguistic approach,
            Cambridge, Mass.: MIT Press [1969], 173-
            186.
Thorne, Barrie [Michigan State Univ.]
   1972   "Girls who say yes to guys who say no: Wom-
            en in the draft resistance movement," paper
            read at the American Sociological Association.
Thorne, Barrie, and Nancy Henley [Harvard Univ.]
   1973   "Sex differences in language, speech, and non-
            verbal communication: An annotated bibliogra-
            phy" (duplicated, 45 pages), Michigan State
            University, Department of Sociology, East
            Lansing, 48823.
Tiedt, Iris M.
   1973   "Sexism in language: an editor's plague,"
            Elementary English 50. 7, (October), 1073-1074.
Tiedt, Pamela, and Robin Semorile
   1973   "Semantic discrepancies," Elementary English
            50. 7, (October), 1065-1066, 1074.

Toth, Emily
    1970   "How can a woman MAN the barricades?: or
                linguistic sexism up against the wall," Women:
                A Journal of Liberation 2:1 (Fall), 57.
Trager, George
    1962   "A scheme for the cultural analysis of sex,"
                Southwestern Journal of Anthropology 18:2
                (Summer), 114-18.
Trombley, Barbara Jean
                "Dictionaries, language, and discrimination,"
                pamphlet (Houghton Mifflin) [on the Ameri-
                can Heritage School Dictionary].
Trudgill, Peter
    1972   "Sex, covert prestige and linguistic change in
                the urban British English of Norwich," Lan-
                guage in Society 1:2 (October), 179-195.
    1974   The social differentiation of English in Nor-
                wich, Cambridge Studies in Linguistics 13
                (New York: Cambridge University Press).
Tucker, Susie E.
    1967   "Women's usage," in Protean shape: a
                study in eighteenth-century vocabulary and
                usage, London: University of London, The
                Athlone Press, pp. 78-80.

Uhlenbeck, C. C.
    1932   Review of Gerlach Royen, "Die nominalen
                Klassifikations-systeme in den Sprachen der
                Erde," International Journal of American Lin-
                guistics 7. 1-2, 94-96 (see Royen).

Vachek, Josef
    1964   "Notes on gender in Modern English," Sborník
                Prací Filosofické Fakulty Brněnské University,
                A 12, 189-194.
Varda One
    19??   "Manglish" (mimeo, 7 pages), Everywoman
                Pub. Co., 1043 B West Washington Blvd.
                Venice, Cal. 90291.

Warshay, Diana W.
    1972   "Sex differences in language style," in Con-
                stantina Safilios-Rothschild, ed., Toward a

sociology of women, Lexington, Mass. : Xerox College Publishing, 3-9.

1973 "The effects of marital status and age on sex differences in language style, " paper read at the IXth International Congress of Anthropological and Ethnological Sciences, Chicago.

Wentworth, Harold, and Stuart Berg Flexner, eds.
1960 "Preface" (by Flexner) to Dictionary of American slang, New York: Thomas Y. Crowell, vi-xv.

White, Toni L. [Candler School of Theology]
19?? "A feminine word to the men of God. "

Whittaker, James O., and Robert D. Meade
1967 "Sex of the communicator as a variable in source credibility, " Journal of social psychology 72. 1, 27-34.

Whorf, Benjamin Lee
ca. 1937 "Grammatical categories, " Language 21:1 (January-March 1945), reprinted in John B. Carroll, ed., Language, thought, and reality: selected writings of Benjamin Lee Whorf, Cambridge, Mass.: MIT Press, 1962, 87-101.

Wise, C. M.
1951 "'Chiefess'--a Hawaiian word, " American Speech 26:2, 116-121.

Withington, Robert
1937 "'Lady', 'woman', and 'person', " American Speech 12:2 (April), 117-121.
1937 "Woman-Lady, " American Speech 12:3 (October), 235.

Wood, Marion M.
1966 "The influence of sex and knowledge of communication effectiveness on spontaneous speech," Word 22:1-3 (April-December), 112-137.

Woolf, Virginia
1929 A room of one's own, New York: Harcourt, Brace and World, 1957.

Yamasawa, Kayoko, and Takae Takamizu
1969 "Women's language: east and west, " Collected essays by the members of the faculty, No. 13, Kyoritsu, Japan: Kyoritsu Women's Junior College, 140-156.

Zerffi, William A. C.
1957 "Male and female voices, " American Medical

Association Archives of Otolaryngology 65,
pp. 7-10.
Zimmerman, Don H. and Candy West [University of California
  at Santa Barbara]
    1973   "Conversational order and sexism: a conver-
              gence of theoretical and substantive problems. "

NAME INDEX

Abarbanel, Albert 153, 160
Abercrombie, David 157
Abrahams, Roger D. 160
Agnew, Spiro 84
Alasdair, Mary 121
Alyeshmerni, Mansoor 80, 158
Anderson, George K. 164
Anderson, Paul S. 65
Annan, Noel Gilroy 123, 163, 164
Argyle, Michael 162, 165
Aristotle 13
Aston, W. G. 163
Atwood, E. Bagby 154
Austen, Jane 119, 121, 123
Austin, George A. 81
Austin, William M. 109-110

Bach, Emmon 158
Baecklund, Astrid 164
Bailey, Rosalie Fellows 153
Baker, Sidney J. 164
Balfour, Henry 162
Bánhidi Zoltán 154
Baratz, Joan C. 159
Barbara, Dominick A. 162
Barber, Charles 157
Bardwick, Judith M. 156
Bart, Pauline 151
Beauvoir, de see de Beauvoir
Beinhauer, Werner 162
Bennet, Edward M. 157
Bergman, Ingmar 127
Berko, Jean 155
Bierce, Ambrose 154

Bird, Caroline 164
Birdwhistell, Ray L. 115, 161, 162
Blood, Doris 156, 165
Blount, Ben G. 157
Blount, Thomas 82
Boas, Franz 82, 158
Bolinger, Dwight 157
Bosmajian, Haig A. 166
Bradstreet, Anne 117
Brazelton, T. Berry 154
Brend, Ruth M. 157
Breton, Raymond 14
Brilliant, Richard 162
Brinton, Daniel 150
Brontë, Charlotte 118-119, 121
Brontë, Emily 118-119, 121
Broverman, Inge K. 150
Brower, Reuben A. 159
Brown, Roger 82, 153
Bruner, Jerome S. 81, 158
Buck, Pearl S. 126, 164
Bullowa, Margaret 154
Burr, Elizabeth 155
Butler, Samuel 121, 163

Cammack, Floyd M. 161
Carroll, John B. 157, 159
Carroll, Lewis 97
Caso, Alfonso 151
Catford, J. C. 150
Cawdry, Robert 82
Chatterji, Suniti Kumar 156
Chaucer 30, 128
Chesterfield, Earl of 14, 102
Chesterton, Gilbert K. 119, 163

191

GENERAL INDEX